REALITY
UNVEILED

REALITY UNVEILED

THE HIDDEN KEYS OF EXISTENCE THAT WILL
TRANSFORM YOUR LIFE (AND THE WORLD)

ZIAD MASRI

ISBN Paperback: 978-0-9986324-1-4

For every person who has felt the call of the heart
and thought, "there must be more to life."

CONTENTS

INTRODUCTION
WHAT YOU SEEK IS SEEKING YOU

You picked up this book for a reason. Whether you're looking for personal transformation, success, peace, joy, or love, you are a seeker of truth. You may not label yourself as such, but nevertheless something inside of you searches unceasingly. And while that search can seem endless at times, take hope, because this is not a one-way quest. For as the great Sufi poet, Rumi, so wisely said, "What you seek is seeking you."

This profound truth will become clearer as you read through this book. Questions that you might have always had, which perhaps you thought would always go unanswered, will be answered. A breathtaking reality, which you might have always hoped could be real, will reveal itself. And every pain and struggle you've ever endured will suddenly start to make sense, as you understand the deeper purpose behind our existence and why we're here.

Each of us feels lost and confused at times. We might think we have it all figured out, and then something comes along and turns our world upside down. Yet even when life is seemingly right side up, we often feel something is missing: An internal nagging feeling, telling us that even when we're at our happiest,

1

we're not complete. It's not always so subtle either, sometimes feeling like a gaping void. And we try to fill it in any way we can—money, success, relationships, and so on in an attempt to feel complete—but it's a bottomless pit. So we stay hungry.

Many of us feel a strong sense of disconnection too. And, ironically, the more connected we become with the help of technology and social media, the more disconnected we often feel—from others, our life, and our very selves. The world echoes this disconnection, as all the poverty, violence, and destruction can feel overwhelming and leave us wondering what's the point of it all. It can seem like no matter what we do, we'll never be truly happy and find what we're looking for on this strange journey called life.

But our seeking is not futile. And when we're truly ready, we find what we've always been looking for. I have been on a 15-year journey of self-discovery, and even though the path has been anything but easy, the proverbial light at the end of the tunnel does exist. Even though I had to push and struggle, and felt utterly hopeless at times, looking back I can see that what I was looking for was not only there all along, but silently guiding me each step of the way. I realized that the void inside can't be filled; not because it's too vast, but because it's an *illusion*. It's not really there. And if you open your heart and mind and come with me on this journey, this truth is awaiting your discovery.

The Transformation Unfolds

I have divided this book into two parts.

Part I will take you on an adventure, immersing you in a world of wonder, while revealing the evidence that supports every surprising concept. You may have heard of some of the ideas before, but when you see all the incredible evidence come together, piece by piece, it becomes a powerful tool of transformation. Becoming more aware of how the world works on an energetic and spiritual level raises your consciousness, which then allows you to tap into a higher level of functioning. And when that happens a shift in perception takes place, and you suddenly see the world through an empowering new lens.

The other key is integration. So often we'll discover potentially life-changing knowledge, but its only effect is to make us pause momentarily before life rushes back in and distracts us, and we end up relegating the knowledge to the recesses of our minds. But what I offer you here is a cohesive framework, where each concept complements and builds on the one before, bringing together the scattered pieces of a complex puzzle. With this framework in place, everything becomes so much clearer. Your life, the world, the universe, and existence itself begin to make more sense.

In Part II, we take this framework and put it to use in transforming our lives. You can think of Part II as the practical side of the knowledge Part I reveals. It includes "Awakening Practices" designed to raise your level of consciousness and connect you to the hidden beauty within yourself and the very structure of existence. The epilogue then takes everything to an even higher level, as I share a daily awakening practice that has proven to be profoundly transformative.

As everything comes together, you'll see how the hidden truths of reality can be applied to everyday life to create more peace, joy, and true fulfillment, while providing the deep sense of purpose that we're all searching for.

DISCERNMENT ON THE JOURNEY

But before we begin on this adventure of a lifetime, I want you to know that I'm not claiming to have all the answers. What I share is my perspective of the ultimate truth, based on my own (sometimes extraordinary) life experiences, and what I've come to discern to be true after extensively researching non-mainstream science and spirituality. As such, there will inevitably be some things that run so counter to your current belief system that you just won't be able to accept them. That's completely fine, but try not to use that as an excuse to throw out everything else. As with anything new, take what resonates with you and leave the rest. Even if you only take a few concepts from this book, they can still be profoundly transformative. Each hidden aspect of reality, along with its practical application, is that powerful. So make a commitment to continue reading, even if you come across some things you can't instantly accept to be true. You may find evidence in a later chapter that changes your perspective, or you may continue to reject one thing but find great value in another. Either way, it will pay great dividends to continue reading with an open mind.

But that brings us to another issue, which is the power of beliefs. While you should be discerning and not accept anything just because I (or anyone else) said it, it's just as important to be willing to openly examine your own beliefs. Are they truly yours? Did you come to them by objectively investigating the world around you or do you simply believe them to be true because that's what you were taught at an early age by your parents, teachers, and society at large? If we're honest, we often find that many of the things that we believe to be true, and seemingly self-evident, are actually a product of conditioning and not necessarily self-discerned truths. As such, whenever you encounter resistance while reading this book, I'd suggest taking a moment to pause and ask whether you know the absolute truth based on personal experience, or whether you only think you know because that's what you learned early on and have held to be true because you have never challenged it with contrary evidence. This discernment exercise will raise your consciousness in and of itself, because you'll be approaching life from a more empowered standpoint, instead of being the unknowing captive of your unquestioned beliefs.

Finally, I hope this book will become a living resource that you can share with others so that they too can transform their lives. But please keep in mind that it's not about trying to convince others that you're right and they're wrong. Each of us must remain vigilant over our need to be right and convert others to our belief system or worldview, and instead offer them the chance to decide for themselves, free of our judgments over whether they accept it or not.

Now, having said that, let's delve into the enthralling (and often surprising) secrets of existence that have the power to immediately transform your life and the world you live in.

PART I
LIFTING THE VEIL

"You are the universe experiencing itself."

– ALAN WATTS

CHAPTER 1

THE ILLUSION
WE CALL REALITY

"Reality is merely an illusion,
albeit a very persistent one."

– ALBERT EINSTEIN

Does it strike you as odd that Einstein, one of the greatest minds the world has ever known, described reality as "merely an illusion"? Was he simply referring to some esoteric concept or perhaps speaking metaphorically? Or was he actually revealing one of life's biggest secrets to us?

As you're about to discover, there is a staggering amount of scientific evidence that proves that the reality we perceive with our senses is actually a highly convincing illusion. That, as William Shakespeare so eloquently put it, "All the world's a stage, and all the men and women merely players." And even this well-known quote may have been meant very literally by Shakespeare, whose genius likely extended beyond the written word to a deep understanding of the hidden nature of reality. So let's start by looking at what most of us perceive as we go about our daily lives.

THE MISLEADING FIELD OF PERCEPTION THAT WE CALL "SEEING"

Living life by the adage that "seeing is believing" makes sense, doesn't it? Observing the external world with our own two eyes seems to be our proof that there is a very real reality "out there." Our eyesight clearly tells us that this world is real and solid, and so perhaps it seems more logical and scientific to doubt the existence of anything that we can't see.

Until, that is, we start getting curious about how our eyes actually work. Because that's when we start to realize that there may be more to the world than "meets the eye."

When we look at a given area or place, instead of seeing all there is to see there, we are actually seeing a tiny frequency range within the electromagnetic spectrum called "visible light." As you can see from Figure 1.1 below, there are many different forms of energy that are literally invisible to the eye. They exist all around us, occupying the same space and time, and can be measured with scientific instruments—but we can't see them. Some scientists even now state that this *entire* electromagnetic spectrum (of which light is only a tiny part) actually represents only 0.005 percent of all the energy in the universe. Even the "physical universe" that we can detect makes up only 4 percent of it, according to many astronomers.[1]

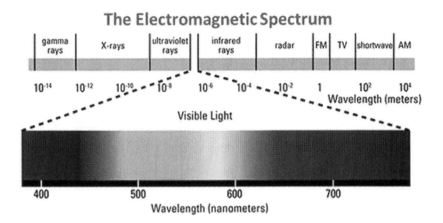

Figure 1.1 The electromagnetic spectrum

Pause to consider the implications of this staggering fact. It's telling us that all physical existence that we can see—in the form of rocks, trees, animals, humans, planets, stars, entire galaxies, and so on—is only a tiny fraction of what actually exists based on the gravitational effects astronomers see this hidden universe causing. Quite literally, at least 96 percent of "reality" is simply invisible to us. We perceive so little and yet think this is all there is.

So what does this mean exactly? It means that if we open our minds to what we can't see, then we might need to rethink how much we know about reality. When we realize that virtually everything we currently believe about the nature of existence comes from trusting our senses, and yet those very senses can only detect an infinitesimally small portion of reality, we become open to questioning if we actually know the nature of reality at all.

It's not easy to question something when our senses report that it's real and it's all there is. One day we were born and started perceiving the world. It's all we've ever known. And so surely if we perceive it in a certain way, and every one of the billions of other people like us perceive it in a certain way, then it must be that way, right?

Not so fast. Ponder something, if you will. You, I, and all those billions of people were born with a body that is a biological receiver/transmitter that decodes the world via our senses to show us "reality." But how do we know that this body isn't just showing us an extremely limited version of the greater reality? Indeed, the body is showing us only what it is *programmed to see*, much like a computer can only show us what it is programmed to display. And yet we have been trying to use what it shows us as "proof" of the nature of reality. Do you see the faulty logic at play here?

We're using the very thing that is programmed to show us only a tiny aspect of reality as proof that this tiny aspect of reality is how things are or that this is all there is. Before moving on, pause for a moment and really think about this.

If we programmed a computer to perform a small set of mathematical functions, could we use its output to prove that this is all the math that exists? Of course not, and the body is the same: it can only see what it is programmed to see. When we look through our eyes, we are not seeing reality but *merely decoding information in the form of light* and literally blind to everything else. We know there are countless other energies and frequencies that are just as "real," but the human body (our receiver/transmitter) is not built to perceive them. For example, right now there are radio waves and ultraviolet waves all around you, but you can't perceive them. And as we've discovered, these energies are just a small part of the electromagnetic spectrum (from which you only perceive visible light), which itself represents possibly only 0.005 percent of all the energy that exists. So just imagine how little of reality you actually perceive. Your body was designed to decode only a tiny portion of what exists. And as you'll see later in the book, there are *entire realms* that coexist in the same "space" as us, but similarly we're unable to perceive them through any of our senses.

But before we get to that fascinating subject, let's turn to the strange science of quantum physics and see what it tells us about our so-called reality.

SCIENTIFIC REVOLUTIONS

Niels Bohr, one of the founding fathers of quantum physics and winner of the Nobel Prize in 1922, echoed Einstein when he said,

"If quantum mechanics hasn't profoundly shocked you, you haven't understood it yet. Everything we call real is made of things that cannot be regarded as real."

But what does this have to do with the science that we learned at school and which the majority of the world believes? Unfortunately, very little. Scratch beneath the surface and we discover that mainstream science fails badly when trying to explain the true nature of reality. Yet despite that, it is the science that is "sold" to us. So let's delve into the new science of quantum physics and see what it tells us about the nature of reality.

The first scientific revolution began in the 16th century and produced such household names as Copernicus, Galileo, and Newton. This era came to be known as "classical physics," and it looks at external reality as solid, stable, and machinelike in its predictable behavior.

This science is still taught in schools and is accurate for describing the physical world that is visible to the naked eye, which is why most people think it's the only science in which we can have faith. But when we examine the subatomic world, we find that all the rules of classical physics become completely and utterly *violated*.

In short, things that are absolutely not supposed to happen, given our standard scientific understanding, all of a sudden start happening with astonishing regularity. And so it was that the 20th-century physicists like Niels Bohr and Albert Einstein—as well as many others like Erwin Schrodinger, Max Planck, and David Bohm, to name but a few—were absolutely awestruck at what they found when they started studying the tiny world of subatomic particles.

One of the most astounding discoveries is what has been referred to as the "dual nature" of particles. Classical physics tells us that particles (such as electrons or photons of light) are solid, and behave much like tiny marbles. But when quantum physicists devised the now infamous "double-slit" experiment[2] to study their behavior, they were utterly baffled.

To summarize, the experiment consists of firing electrons, one by one, at a wall with two slits in it, and observing the pattern that emerges on the other side. Based on classical physics, we would expect the supposedly solid electrons to go through one slit or the other, and end up creating a pattern of two vertical lines, as shown in figure 1.2.

Figure 1.2 Expected observation of the double-split experiment

Strangely, this is not what occurs. Instead of forming two vertical lines, the particles end up forming the interference pattern depicted in figure 1.3.

Figure 1.3 Actual observation of the double-split experiment

According to classical physics, such an interference pattern can only occur if a *wave* is being fired at the wall, not a particle, as seen in figure 1.4. As the peak of one wave overlaps with the peak of another, they amplify each other, and as their troughs overlap they cancel each other.

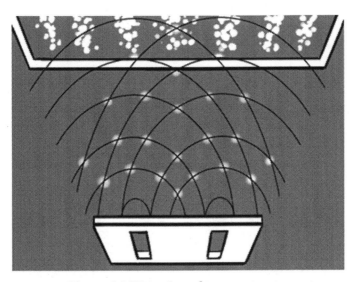

Figure 1.4 Wave interference pattern

But how could single electrons fired one at a time create an interference pattern that can only possibly be created by waves?

Sophisticated mathematical analysis showed that the same electron would not only have to go through both slits at the same time, but also go through neither slit, and only the right slit, and only the left slit. Obviously, that makes no sense at all, which is why the experiment left the scientists baffled.

To unravel this mystery of seemingly impossible math and physics, they decided to set up a measuring device to see which slit each particle was actually going through. Figure 1.5 shows the baffling results.

Figure 1.5 The effect of introducing a measuring device in the double-slit experiment

When the electrons are watched with a measuring device, all of a sudden they start acting like solid particles again, instead of like a wave! It seems impossible that the electrons are consciously aware of being watched, and so choose to act like we would expect them to in that moment, but that is precisely what the results indicated.

And with that, scientists were thrust into the strange world of quantum physics, suddenly realizing that far from the relatively simplistic and mechanistic ideas of Newtonian physics, we find that supposedly solid, inanimate particles actually exist as non-solid waves of potentiality that come into and out of physical existence based on their interaction with consciousness.

So what does this really mean? How can supposedly physical particles pop into and out of physical reality like this, which classical science tells us is not possible?

MUCH ADO ABOUT NOTHING: THE IMMATERIALITY OF THE MATERIAL WORLD

Study quantum physics beyond a cursory level, and you'll reach the inescapable conclusion that the reason physical particles behave in such a strange way is because they're *not* physical at all.

We know that everything in the universe is made up of atoms, which are usually depicted as having a big solid nucleus with electrons spinning around it in neat orbits. But when quantum physicists took a closer look, they discovered that there's actually *nothing* really there. In fact, they discovered that 99.9999999999996 percent of the atom is literally empty space.[3] The nucleus seems to be solid but is so infinitely small as to effectively not be there. The rest is essentially a physical void. It's like looking at an invisible tornado-like vortex of energy with infinitely tiny particles seemingly popping into existence one moment and then out the next, with the whole thing being as insubstantial as a puff of smoke. It can't actually be touched because, as it turns out, there's literally nothing there to touch.

In fact, it has been calculated that if you took the entire population of the Earth, all seven billion of us, and removed all the empty space from all of our combined atoms, the entire human race would fit into a *single sugar cube*.[4] Now if that doesn't boggle your mind, then I don't know what will—so much for a solid world.

But if there is such an infinitesimally small amount of "solid" matter in the universe, then why does everything look and feel so undeniably solid to us?

Our senses tell us that everything is solid. Just pick up a rock and try to understand how there's actually nothing solid to it and that it's all empty space in reality. It's difficult to imagine. The secret is in the electrostatic field that surrounds the atoms (i.e., the orbiting electron cloud). When two atoms come close together, their electron clouds repel each other so that the nuclei never actually touch. But you, holding that rock in your hand, *feel* that it's very solid, as if you're touching it. What's actually happening is that you are feeling the sensation of electrostatic repulsion as your hand's atoms come into one 100-millionth of a centimeter of that of the rock's.[5]

The same thing happens any time you "touch" any apparently solid object. There is *nothing* solid there to touch. If you are reading this book in your hand, then your hand is not actually touching it. Rather, the nonphysical tornado-like clouds of atoms are repelling one another at unimaginably tiny distances so that you have the illusion of touching something solid. That apparent solidity of touch is all coming from the sensation of the electrostatic repulsion between the atoms. Indeed, you're not even touching the chair you're sitting on; instead, you're hovering one 100-millionth of a centimeter above it, feeling it so solidly under you due to the atomic repulsion between its atoms and yours.

And as far as sight—that is, how absolutely solid everything *looks*—remember that we are dealing with an atomic world so small that you need highly sophisticated microscopes to see it. So it's not a stretch to imagine how non-solid clouds of energy, which have magnetic forces to hold them together, can be packed so incredibly close together so as to *seem* like one solid object (like a human body or a rock), but in reality be nothing more than a very convincing *illusion*.

And so now we come full circle back to Einstein and see why (and there were many other scientific reasons) he so famously claimed that reality is merely an illusion. He was stating the literal truth. There *is* no physical reality. We, and everything else in the universe, don't actually have any physical structure!

As we're about to see, this is all a very convincing illusion being projected from a "dimension" completely outside time and space.

CHAPTER 2
CONSCIOUSNESS ALTERS REALITY

"I regard consciousness as fundamental.
I regard matter as derivative from consciousness.
We cannot get behind consciousness. Everything that
we talk about, everything that we regard as existing,
postulates consciousness."

– MAX PLANCK

To recap what we've covered so far, non-mainstream modern science has now shown us that:

1. Most of what exists in the universe (what is all around us and even occupying the same "space" as us) cannot be seen given how our biological receiver/transmitter that we call our body is built—that is, it's specifically programmed to see and experience only a tiny aspect of reality and to literally be blind to all else.

2. All that we do see and touch is not as it seems, having no solidity whatsoever when examined at the smallest levels.

Instead, matter seems to act simultaneously as waves of energy and as seemingly solid particles that are continuously popping into and out of material existence at a rate too fast for us to detect.

Now the very interesting realization that comes about when you integrate these two facts is that the idea of an objective reality that we can observe *separate from us* completely falls apart. In fact, the inescapable conclusion from all of these scientific discoveries is that "separation" is the biggest illusion of all. In reality, quantum physicists have discovered (much to their shock) that everything is connected as *one* thing that is merely appearing to be many things.

IT'S ALL ONE

Think about it. If it's known that all matter has a dual nature, both acting as a seemingly solid particle (although never actually quite being solid) and as a wave of energy, where does one wave end and the next wave begin?

Alan Watts, the mid-20th-century British contemporary philosopher, perhaps said it best when he stated, "You and I are all as much continuous with the physical universe as a wave is continuous with the ocean."

The ocean is a helpful metaphor here, as we can see seemingly separate waves, and even identify one wave as being different and apart from another wave. And yet, can we truly say they are separate? Can we actually define where one wave ends and the rest of the ocean, along with all the other waves, begin? Are they not part of the same ocean and inextricably linked to such a point that they meld into one another and join together as one?

That may be clear to see in an ocean due to the nature of water, which is a continuous fluid. It's harder to see perhaps when we're looking at rocks, trees, animals, and humans. But we now know that our eyes deceive us. What we see as solid and separate is not actually so, but rather seemingly separate waves of energy within the ocean of universal energy known as the "quantum field."

It is this quantum field that is the source of all things in material reality. It is known by many names, including the "Source Field," "Superstring Field," and "Unified Field," but essentially refers to the same thing: the place from which the seemingly solid material world springs and in which it resides.

But make no mistake: it's all One thing—an ocean of energy that collapses into seemingly separate forms that we call stars and planets and animals and trees and human beings, giving them the temporary *illusion* of solidity and separation from their purely energetic source. But they always remain one with one another and their source. In fact, if we were able to alter the way the brain decodes information, then instead of seeing separate people and buildings and mountains, we would simply see interconnected waves of energy vibrating at different frequencies, not so different from the movie *The Matrix*, when Neo starts seeing reality in computer code. Indeed, it has been reported that, in rare instances, some people's brains are wired differently from birth,[6] and they see the world as a continuous interconnected wave of energy, instead of the physical illusion of separation that it seems to be.

THE PRISON OF PERCEPTION

It can be difficult to wrap our minds around all of this because perception can seem so incredibly convincing. But the key to awakening to the true nature of reality is to realize that perception, when taken at face value, is in fact a prison. As Goethe, one of the great thinkers in history so astutely pointed out, "The best slave is the one who thinks he is free."

And yet such is the status of the majority of humanity. We are slaves to our perceptions while thinking they make us free to see reality as it is. Only when we face the undeniable fact that perception merely shows us what it is *programmed* to see can we make the leap to look beyond the limitations of the five senses toward ultimate reality.

And what is ultimate reality? One of mankind's greatest geniuses and inventors, Nikola Tesla, gave us a clue when he said, "If you want to know the secrets of the universe, think in terms of energy, frequency and vibration."

Although we'll discuss the spiritual side of ultimate reality in the next chapter, on the "physical" side, ultimate reality is simply that everything is pure energy. And once again, while this may be hard to fathom when everything seems so solid and we can't actually *see* this energy, we must remember that we can't use the very instrument (the human body), which is literally programmed only to show us the "prison cell," to decide if anything exists beyond it.

Now don't get me wrong. I'm not saying that the body is a bad thing or faulty in any way. There is a specific and useful reason that the body is programmed in this way, which we'll also cover in a later chapter. I'm simply saying that if we place all our trust in our five senses, then we will think we are free while in reality we are mere prisoners of our severely limited perception.

BEYOND THE ILLUSION OF SEPARATION

The solution to escaping the prison of perception is to let go of the idea of separation, regardless of how real your senses are telling you it is, and to think more in line with what modern science (and as we'll see in coming chapters, also ancient spirituality) tells us reality actually is. This can essentially be captured in one idea: Unity. Everything is unified. Everything is One. Separation is the true illusion.

And once again, Albert Einstein left us with the undeniable proof with his most famous formula: $E=mc^2$. Most people have heard of this equation, but what does it really mean? Very simply, matter and energy are actually one and the same.

Think about that. We are being given proof and validation by one of history's greatest geniuses that all matter *is* energy. Not that matter has energy. But that it *is* energy. And if it's all energy, then it can't be separate. Energy doesn't have a cutoff point where it ends and another separate energy begins. Just like the waves of the ocean, it's all connected. It's all One. The only thing that changes is the rate at which it vibrates—that is, its frequency. And isn't that what that other great genius of our time, Nikola Tesla, is telling us when he asks us to "think in terms of energy, frequency and vibration"?

I hope you're seeing now how everything adds up. We know about these equations and we've heard the quotes. But rarely do we bring it all together and understand the true implications. Rarely do we think about what it's *actually telling us*. But the answers are all right there in front of our eyes. The world we think we live in is nothing but an illusory aspect of our perceptions. We are in *The Matrix* without even realizing it. And only when we put all the evidence together do we get a clear picture of the true nature of reality.

EVIDENCE FROM EVERYDAY LIFE

Up until now we've discussed things from a purely scientific level that may be hard for any non-scientist to truly relate to. But there is plenty of scientific evidence that doesn't require a PhD to be understood. In fact, most of us can easily relate to it, making it all the more powerful.

MASS MEDITATION TRANSFORMS MASS REALITY

In David Wilcock's excellent book *The Source Field Investigations: The Hidden Sciences and Lost Civilizations Behind the 2012 Prophecies*,[7] he cites one particularly important study that really stayed with me.

In 1978, a scientifically controlled study was conducted on a group of 7,000 expert meditators. The group meditated together for a period of three weeks, focusing on thoughts of love and peace. Incredibly, it was found that during this period, there was a significant drop in *global* crime rates by an average of 16 percent. Global suicide rates and automobile accidents were also reduced. Most astonishing of all, there was a 72 percent reduction in global terrorist activity!

Think about it. Just 7,000 people decreased the crime, suicide, accident, and terrorism rates of the entire globe and, more incredibly, did it using nothing more than their minds! Bear in mind, this was a controlled scientific study that took into account every possible variable, including weather, holidays, global events, and anything else that could have caused such a decline, and they were all ruled out. There was nothing distinctly different about this period as compared to any other—except for these 7,000 meditators focusing on love and world peace.

And of course by now you know why this is possible: Separation is an illusion. Although it may seem each one of us is separate from the next, and that our thoughts are individual to us, nothing could be further from the truth. Beyond the deception of perception, we are like waves in the ocean of humanity, all connected as One basic energy.

When we meditate or pray in concert, we can create what's called "energetic coherence." We looked at how waves act in Chapter 1 (see figure 1.4), and noted how scientists have observed that wave coherence—whether they are ocean waves or waves of energy—creates large amplitude waves, while a lack of it creates a cancelling-out effect. These 7,000 meditators were able to build coherence in their thoughts and emotions (which, like physical matter, are forms of energy), thus creating large energetic waves in the ocean of universal energy. The rest of the world's population, while completely unaware of the meditators, were directly affected by this energy because it is the very source that gives them physical form and life—that is, they are a part of it and one with it.

Even if the mechanics of this phenomenon aren't fully clear, we would still have to come to the inescapable conclusion that reality is not as it seems because we have been led to believe by classical physics that everything is separate and that we can't change something other than by exerting a physical force upon it (this is what we learned in school and what is still being taught for the most part). This experiment blows that model of reality out of the water. Quite simply, what happened in the mass meditation study should not have happened given our classical understanding of science. And yet it did. That's because separation is an illusion, and the reality is that everything is One—One field of energy, appearing to be a multitude of physical things.

It's also important to note that this experiment was not a one-time thing. Hundreds like it have been performed in various capacities, and the results have been consistent in their significance. Time and time again, we see things that should not be happening under the model of the world we've been told we live in.

And in case you thought that only humans are connected by the same fundamental energy, think again.

WATER RESPONDS DIRECTLY TO OUR THOUGHTS AND WORDS

We're told that water is an inanimate element, something that exists as separate and apart from us, and which can only be changed if put through some kind of machine or chemical process. However in the mid 1990s Dr. Masaru Emoto, a Japanese scientist, decided to see whether thoughts, words, and music could have any effect on water. While his non-mainstream methods have come under criticism by some Western scientists and skeptics, we must remember that anyone who threatens our view of reality is likely to be attacked and face a battle to have their work discredited, and we must remain vigilant to not quickly dismiss the results.

Dr. Emoto's method involved:

- Showing words to the water
- Showing pictures to the water
- Playing music to the water
- Praying to the water

After that, he froze the water and then observed the frozen crystals under the microscope. Now, if you told most people that you were showing a word or picture to water, they might think you were crazy. But what Dr. Emoto found was nothing short of astounding.

Words and Water

The following series of images shows the effects of words on water:

Figure 2.1 Frozen water crystals after being shown the words, "Thank you"

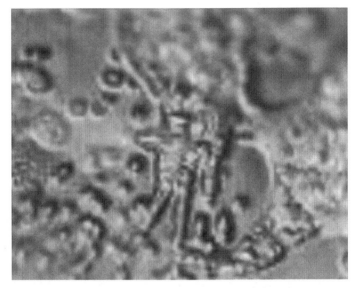

Figure 2.2 Frozen water crystals after being shown the phrase, "You disgust me"

Figure 2.3 Frozen water crystals after being shown the word, "Truth"

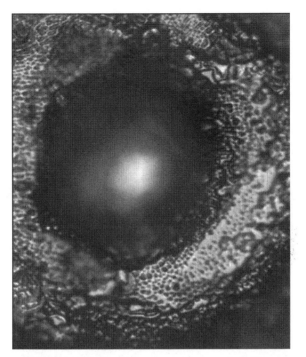

Figure 2.4 Frozen water crystals after
being shown the word, "Evil"

Please note what we're looking at here. This is the *same* water with
the only difference being the word it was shown! Before analyzing
the staggering implications of this, let's continue with our next set
of results from Dr. Emoto's research.

Music and Water

The following two images show the effect of particular music on
water crystals.

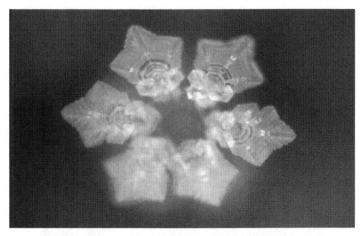

Figure 2.5 Frozen water crystals after being played, *Imagine* by John Lennon

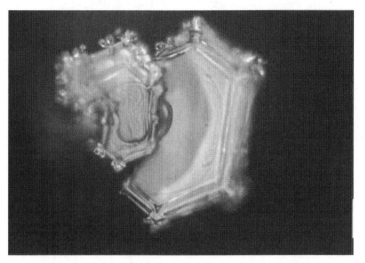

Figure 2.6 Frozen water crystals after being played *Heartbreak Hotel* by Elvis Presley

Note that Lennon's song *Imagine* is about peace, unity, and love, while Presley's *Heartbreak Hotel* is obviously about more negative subjects.

Prayer and Water

The following images show the effect of prayer on water. Figure 2.7 shows polluted water taken from a Japanese dam, and its frozen crystals look asymmetrical (or what we would call ugly). But after the Buddhist prayer was offered to the water and the water was refrozen, the crystals displayed an absolutely stunning pattern with incredible symmetry, as shown in figure 2.8.

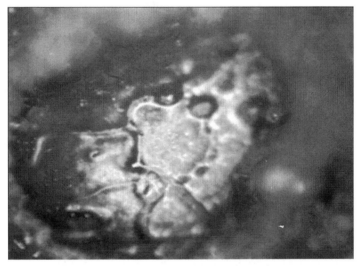

Figure 2.7 Frozen crystals of dam
water before prayer

Figure 2.8 Frozen crystals
of dam water after prayer

Now think about this for a moment. As logical, rational human beings, we've always been taught that inanimate objects and elements can't change their form based on thoughts and words. This is impossible in a Newtonian version of the world. The water is supposed to exist distinctly apart from us. It is supposed to have its own separate existence, and it is not supposed to be alive in any way to respond to thoughts and words like humans can. And yet, the evidence is as clear as day. It *does* respond.

In fact, it responds more directly and beautifully than any one of us could have ever imagined by changing its very structure to reflect the *energy* of the words or thoughts. Yes, even words and thoughts, which we tend to think of as insubstantial and essentially nothing, are the very same energy as everything else.

In fact, here's water directly reacting to Martin Luther King Jr.'s "I have a dream" speech delivered in 1963, to produce a complex and beautiful pattern!

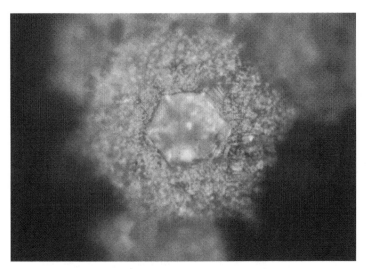

Figure 2.9 Dam water after being played Martin Luther King Jr. speech

We've now seen more direct evidence that literally *everything* is unified energy, appearing to be many different and separate things, but in fact remaining One beneath the surface of the illusion.

And with that realization now firmly in place and the bars of the prison of perception starting to disintegrate, let's venture on to unite the physical with the spiritual. As you're about to see, they're simply two sides of the same coin.

CHAPTER 3

SCIENCE MEETS SPIRITUALITY

"Get over it, and accept the inarguable conclusion.
The universe is immaterial—mental and spiritual."

– RICHARD CONN HENRY

It was the 19th-century German philosopher Arthur Schopenhauer who said that all truth passes through three distinct stages. First, it is ridiculed. Second, it is violently opposed. Third, it is accepted as being self-evident.

When the notion that the Earth is round was put forth at a time when it was generally believed to be flat, at first the idea was mocked. Anyone espousing the idea was considered naive, even crazy. When more scientific proof emerged, however, violent opposition arose. People literally lost their lives for holding such an "insane" belief. Now it was too much of a threat to people's belief systems to be met simply with ridicule; it had to be viciously attacked in order to maintain the perceived comfort and safety of the status quo. Of course, the truth can only be held back for so long, and eventually it became accepted as self-evident that the Earth is indeed round.

These same stages are occurring in the world today regarding the ultimate nature of reality. As discussed in the previous chapters, the material world is far different than we think it is—it is an illusion in every sense of the word. But even as modern scientists are proving this over and over unequivocally, it is currently being met with both ridicule and violent opposition, as physicist Tim Folger describes in his article *Quantum Shmantum:*

"Despite the unrivaled empirical success of quantum theory, the very suggestion that it may be literally true as a description of nature is still greeted with cynicism, incomprehension and even anger."[8]

Yet, in 10, 20, or 50 years, people may look back at this period in human history and wonder how we could have refused to believe the obvious truth, in the same way we perceive those who refused to believe such a seemingly self-evident fact that the Earth is round.

It's important to note, however, that everything our senses scream at us tells us that the Earth is *flat.* We can't see the curvature of the earth. We've likely never seen it from space with our own eyes to "know" that it's actually round. But what we do see is the direct observational and scientific proof that it is round. We know that if we travel in one direction, and keep going, we will eventually end up back where we started. And because of this, we can *infer* the reality of a round Earth despite what our perception shows us and tells us to think. In this way, we can use evidence to override the limitations of our perceptions.

And with the subject of the nature of reality, the evidence is all around us and needs to be used to infer the true nature of the physical—and as we're about to see, the spiritual—realms if we are ever to break free from being slaves to our perceptions and limiting beliefs. All that is needed is an open mind and a willingness to let go of the unquestioned trust that we tend to place in our severely limited senses and perceptions. The question to ask is: Are you willing to open up to the possibility that most of what you've believed to be true up until now will ultimately be accepted as self-evidently false, with a truer picture of reality replacing those outdated beliefs?

I ask this question now because the following ideas have the potential to put your long-held beliefs to the test even further. So an open mind, and a courageous willingness to question what we're usually taught about reality and what we take to be the absolute truth, is crucial at this moment.

INFINITE INTELLIGENCE AND THE MIND OF THE UNIVERSE

As we've already seen, many of the genius scientists of our time have discovered the true nature of physical reality, and they are accumulating a massive amount of evidence to be able to make inferences about the true nature of *spiritual* reality.

Many people relegate spirituality to personal faith or a particular religious doctrine, and believe that it is an unquestionable personal thing. And although I'm not here to tell anyone to change his or her faith, unquestioned blind faith can disempower us and leave us susceptible to control.

Opening up spirituality to modern non-mainstream science and the study of empirical evidence makes much sense. Then, if after all the evidence is presented, we still choose to hold on to our beliefs (that were often simply given to us at a young age with no discernment on our part), then at least those beliefs would now not be the blindly accepted doctrines of those who currently rule society—and by extension our minds—but rather self-discerned personal truths that we have *chosen* to accept as empowered individuals.

An Intelligent Creator

And so with that in mind, let's look at what the great physicist Max Planck describes as the "the existence of a conscious and intelligent Mind," and then delve into more empirical evidence to support such a claim.

"All matter originates and exists only by virtue of a force which brings the particles of the atom to vibration. I must assume behind this force the existence of a conscious and intelligent Mind. This Mind is the matrix of all matter."[9]

If we study this quote, we notice that Planck is not just saying that an intelligent consciousness is the force behind matter (which most of us could readily accept, as many people do believe that there is an intelligent Creator of the universe), but rather that this intelligent consciousness *is* the matter—i.e., the illusion of separation exists not only between all matter itself but also *between all matter and its Creator.*

This is the same spiritual principle echoed throughout the ages by all the great masters and enlightened beings that have walked the Earth. We are one with the Creator in a very literal sense, as we are an inseparable part of the infinite, intelligent consciousness that not only brings forth physical reality but also makes up its very fabric. Indeed, the energy that makes up the fabric of existence that we looked at in the first two chapters is nothing but the physical manifestation of the nonphysical consciousness that created it all and maintains its existence.

How else can we explain how water can change its very structure as it reacts to the energy of thoughts and words? How else can we explain how an electron would change its behavior, one time acting as a seemingly solid particle and another time acting as a wave of energy depending on whether it is being observed? If an independent and separate Creator created the universe and filled it with living and inanimate things, then the nonliving things would not respond to the mere thoughts of the livings things. That is what mainstream science and the *misinterpretation* of the holy books in most religions would have us believe.

And yet what if our definition of life is far too limited? What if *everything* is living, in that everything is made up of the consciousness of the Creator? And by direct implication, what if *everything* is aware? What if the water is aware? And what if the electron is aware? Not aware in the same way as the human being is aware, of course, with our ability to reason, but still fundamentally aware on a basic level of existence because it is imbued with the very fuel of awareness—universal consciousness.

And here we come back, in a clearer light, to the quote by Richard Conn Henry, professor of physics and astronomy at Johns Hopkins University: "Get over it, and accept the inarguable conclusion. The universe is immaterial—mental and spiritual."[10]

Keep in mind that this is a scientist talking. Scientists have long been believed to be at odds with spirituality. And yet more and more of them are being forced to accept the inescapable conclusion that everything is mental; everything is aware; everything is spiritual at the fundamental level. There is only One

Mind here, appearing to be many. There is only One universal intelligence manifesting as *seemingly* living and nonliving matter with a separate existence unto itself. As Einstein reminds us, it is all merely a very convincing illusion.

EVERYTHING IS ALIVE: THE SCIENTIFIC PROOF

If you're thinking that this is all merely theory or some new-age philosophy, despite all the evidence I've shared so far, then think again. There is actually mountains of scientific proof that demonstrates how everything is conscious and therefore alive, aware, *and* intimately connected to everything else, acting more as an interconnected conscious being rather than as a bunch of separate and distinct things "out there" in some objective reality apart from its Creator.

In his book *The Source Field Investigations*,[7] David Wilcock brings together hundreds of little-known scientific experiments with mind-bending implications by the world's most brilliant scientists, and ties them all into a cohesive framework that shows how they integrate with and support the conclusions of one another.

Perhaps the reason that we don't often question our belief systems is due to the fact that we are rarely presented with enough evidence in a cohesive and logical manner to genuinely cause us to rethink things. We may hear an interesting fact here, a surprising tale there, and a mysterious unexplained story another time, and each one of these things may make us briefly pause and think for a minute. But before long, we brush it off and continue life as normal with a completely unchanged worldview.

I know this is true because I've experienced it myself. I had periodically heard of many of the unorthodox subjects that I discuss throughout this book, but it wasn't until I had researched everything so extensively as to piece it all together into a cohesive whole to see how each component fits perfectly with (and complements/validates) the others, that it had a lasting and profound influence on how I viewed the world and lived my life.

And with that in mind, let's delve into some more of the fascinating evidence of a living, conscious universe that is all interconnected.

THE PLANTS ARE LISTENING

Dr. Cleve Backster was an interrogation specialist who worked for the CIA and is the author of *Primary Perception*, which describes more than three decades of fascinating research with plants, food cells, bacteria, and human cells.[11]

To summarize his findings, on February 2, 1966, Backster had the idea of hooking up his plant to a polygraph machine (lie detector) to see what would happen. He thought that the plant would exhibit a flat pattern of electrical activity, but was amazed to observe a pattern that was "similar to a reaction pattern typical of a human subject who might have been briefly experiencing the fear of detection."

Surprised, he decided to see if he could make the plant have a fear *reaction* much like you could get from asking a person who is hooked up to a polygraph something that makes him or her feel anxious. It was at that time, about 14 minutes after he had first hooked the plant up to the polygraph machine, that he had the idea of getting a match and burning the plant's leaf. What happened next was so astounding that it forces us to rethink everything we know about the world.

Even though he was about 16 ft. (5m) away from the plant,

and all he'd done is have the *thought* of burning the plant, at that *very moment* the polygraph charts went crazy, indicating that the plant was experiencing a sudden and intense amount of *anxiety*.

Now keep in mind that Backster did nothing more than *think* of burning the plant. He didn't say anything. He didn't touch the plant. He didn't light a match. Nothing in the room had changed whatsoever, except for having the sudden *idea* to burn the plant. And as its electrical pattern on his instruments showed, *it could hear his thoughts.*

In reality, of course, the plant cannot hear, but the point is that it could receive communication via thought, which is just as real as any other energy in the new model of physics we're describing here. And if it could receive thought energy and interpret it to the point that it could react to a fearful thought with fear and anxiety, then it implies that the plant is *conscious*.

In fact, the plant remained in panic mode and spiked hard again when Backster left the room to get a match, reaffirming his intent to burn the plant. And then there was another spike in the polygraph when he lit the match. It was not until he returned the matches to his secretary's desk that the chart finally returned to a normal, calm electrical pattern.

Now ask yourself, how could a "mindless" plant react instantaneously to a person's thoughts? The answer is that it couldn't. The reality, as we have been discussing in detail, is that the plant has a mind. I'm not saying the plant has a *brain*. We tend to think that the physical brain is what gives rise to the mind, and yet as we'll explore later, nothing could be further from the truth. In short, the brain is nothing more than the physical decoder/transmitter mechanism *used* by the nonphysical mind.

And so what is the mind? It is the universal consciousness

that we've been talking about. And the fact that the plant could receive and react to thoughts shows that it is just as much a part of this consciousness as we are. It may not have an evolved brain to think and reason as we do, but it is nonetheless conscious and aware, being interconnected with the very consciousness that imbues us with awareness. The only difference between us and the plant—or any other element or animal for that matter—is our self-awareness and reasoning capability, which they generally lack. But as the scientific results show, far from what we've been taught to believe, *everything* is conscious and aware.

In fact, Backster is not the only one who has conducted incredible experiments with plants. If you want to read more about this fascinating subject and prove to yourself beyond a shadow of a doubt what we've been discussing here, I recommend reading *The Secret Life of Plants: A Fascinating Account of the Physical, Emotional, and Spiritual Relations between Plants and Man* by Peter Tompkins and Christopher Bird.[12] As you can see just from the book's title, it has the potential to completely transform your ideas about the other beings we share this planet with and just how aware and intimately connected to us they actually are.

But the fascinating research doesn't end there. As predicted by quantum physicists, it turns out that everything you can possibly think of is also conscious and aware.

EVERYTHING ELSE IS LISTENING TOO

Dr. Backster didn't stop at plants and the results were nothing short of amazing. For instance, when he hooked up an ordinary chicken egg to the polygraph machine, he observed that it displayed electrical patterns that are, once again, similar to what you'd see if you were looking at a machine that shows the heartbeat of a human being. But eggs aren't supposed to show that kind of electrical activity, are they? And yet that's nothing compared to what he found next. When he took eggs that were placed beside the one he had hooked up to the machine and put those eggs in boiling water, the chart of the egg being studied went crazy, as if the egg was screaming because the other ones were being boiled.

Dr. Backster saw these results over and over again, and the experiment was conducted to the most stringent scientific levels, with the egg being studied having been placed inside a lead-lined box that did not allow any electromagnetic fields to enter—that is, there could have been no external energy whatsoever causing these shocks in the egg's electrical pattern.

Think about this for a moment. No electromagnetic energy could enter the lead box in which the egg was placed, and yet it was *still* showing massive and consistent spikes in electrical energy each time another egg was placed in boiling water. But how could an individual egg possibly "know" that another one was being placed in boiling water? It doesn't have a brain. It shouldn't be alive by any conventional definitions. And even if it were, then how could it have received this information while it was separately encased and completely shielded from all electromagnetic energy and the "outside" world?

I mean, really think about this. The inescapable conclusion is that not only is the supposedly inanimate egg completely conscious and aware but also fundamentally connected to its entire surroundings on a deep energetic level that goes beyond the electromagnetic spectrum and into the unseen and undetected energy. And this energy, as the great physicist Max Planck stated, *is* the "conscious and intelligent Mind that is the matrix of all matter."

And it's not something that is special and specific just to an egg. When Dr. Backster performed highly controlled (and replicable) scientific experiments with yogurt, vegetables, fruit, the cells of raw animal meat, and more, he found they also exhibited the same anxiety spikes precisely at the moment something else in its vicinity was cooked or eaten. And if you're thinking that this applies just to "living" biological matter, then you only need to think back to the experiments with water in Chapter 2, which show that even completely "nonliving" elements exhibit the same reactions to our energy of thought.

But here's something very interesting. David Wilcock reports that Dr. Backster told him that if you pray over your food, being thankful for it and feeling a sense of love, then it somehow accepts its role as providing sustenance for you, and the intense electrical reactions on the polygraph charts *disappear*.

That puts into new scientific light the religious and spiritual teachings that tell us to pray before we eat. Most people, especially those that follow a spiritual path or religious doctrine, may pray before eating in the belief that they should be thankful for what they have been given by a Creator that is separate and external to them. The scientific evidence gives a more profound explanation, however. It's not that we should be thankful that we are being given sustenance by a Creator separate and external to us, but rather that we should be thankful and loving because everything we interact with is ultimately interconnected as One Mind or One Spirit, being illusory projections of the One energy that many people label as "God." That is, the entire physical realm of living and nonliving things is the direct extension of the nonphysical realm of pure, infinite consciousness that *is* the Creator. We, and everything else we interact with, are not separate from the Creator but the expressions of the unified consciousness that the Creator uses to experience Itself. There is only One appearing as many. All separation is merely illusion, even between us and the Infinite Consciousness that is the Creator. And we have the science to prove it.

In the following chapter, we will step back from the grand view of the whole illusion and explore some of the most important aspects within it, and how it ties in directly to the deeper purpose behind existence. It's one thing to understand that reality is an illusion and that everything is One thing in truth. It's a whole other thing to understand why this is the case. And understanding the structure within the illusion gives us a much better understanding of its purpose. Later on in Chapter 6 I'll be tying this knowledge together to explain our ultimate role within it all.

CHAPTER 4

THE PATH OF
THE SOUL

"Don't grieve. Anything you lose
comes round in another form."

– RUMI

If you ask people what they believe, many would say that God
(whom they view to be distinctly outside them as a separate grand
entity) created a solid physical universe, as well as a heaven and a
hell, and that he presides over all of this creation, independent of
it. This is what the holy books seem to say. The atheists and
rationalists, on the other hand, might say that there is only a
random universe and no Creator at all, and that nothing happens
once you die. This is what mainstream science seems to say. And
while I would say that everyone is entitled to their beliefs, I think
it is our duty as empowered human beings to not merely accept
anything blindly just because we happened to be taught it at birth,
but rather to look at what the evidence actually says.

For the atheist or rationalist, that means looking beyond the
five senses and the prison of perception to the unseen order and
conscious intelligence behind all things, which completely

obliterates the classical science that is at the base of their beliefs in a random, non-conscious, non-spiritual universe. For the religiously devout person, that means looking at the evidence that doesn't attempt to disprove the content or source of their books but rather leads to a different and more correct interpretation of them. In both cases, it is important that we become discerning individuals who don't believe anything that we're told blindly, but rather decide for ourselves after studying all the existing evidence and opening our minds to a different view of reality.

ONE LIFE AND THAT'S IT?

One subject that seems to be most accepted by blind faith is what happens after we die. This makes a lot of sense because such a subject seems to be beyond the scope of scientific or empirical study. As such, many of us feel that we have no other option but to completely trust what we've been told by our religious leaders (note: not necessarily the religion itself), spiritual gurus (note: not necessarily the essence of the spirituality itself), or mainstream scientists (note: not necessarily the real science itself).

But what if there *is* ample evidence about what actually happens? What if both the true science *and* the truth at the heart of the spiritual teachings actually tell us the same thing, which happens to be very different from what we've been told about these sources? Once again, it's not so much about having to doubt the source if you are a devout believer (whether in religion, certain spiritual paths, or science), but rather what we've been told about them by the leaders who dictate our beliefs for their own agendas while giving us the *illusion* that we are free individuals who are deciding for ourselves what to believe. So with that in mind, let's look at the evidence and decide for ourselves.

CHILDREN POINT US TO THE TRUTH

Possibly the most incredible and *directly verifiable* proof of what happens after death comes from children who remember their past lives. Many people dismiss the subject of reincarnation without taking the time to look at the massive amount of empirical and scientific evidence that supports it. But as discerning and empowered individuals, we will now examine the evidence and make an informed decision about what to believe. And for those whose religious upbringing tells them that there is only one life and no such thing as reincarnation, I offer the possibility that the "one" life referred to in the religious texts is symbolic of the combination of all earthly lifetimes—i.e., in the beginning you were spirit, then you experience physical life (a multitude of times), and then you return to spirit. Viewed in this way, with all physical lifetimes representing one distinct phase of what the soul experiences, there is no contradiction. But even if you can't accept this possibility immediately, it's a rewarding exercise to gently open your mind to examining the evidence objectively and coming to your own informed decision.

There have been numerous books written on the subject of reincarnation. Entire volumes have been dedicated to it. In fact, some researchers have spent their entire careers investigating it, and none more so than Dr. Ian Stevenson of the Virginia School of Medicine. Dr. Stevenson spent more than 40 years visiting more than 3,000 children who had very detailed and specific past-life memories. A large number of these children were able to tell him the exact names they had in their past lives, the names of their families, and even the names of their friends. All this despite having absolutely no connection whatsoever to those people in this lifetime and sometimes being in completely different geographical areas that would make it impossible for them to have even heard of them. Many could also tell him how and where they had died, and incredibly, not only would it all be proven true upon visiting the relatives of the deceased but there would often be a birthmark on the child in the exact place that a wound had been inflicted on the deceased in a violent death in the previous lifetime.

Time after time, Dr. Stevenson found that the names the children gave him were 100 percent correct. He tracked down their prior lifetime relatives and confirmed that the things the children were claiming were all true. Most astonishingly, perhaps, he noticed that when he visited the alleged past-life relatives and saw pictures of who the children claimed to have been, there was often a remarkable resemblance between them in this lifetime and the last. Dr. Stevenson had collected so much undeniable data that he finally published a book detailing it all called *Children Who Remember Previous Lives: A Question of Reincarnation* (2001).[13]

Among some of the cases that have been extensively researched by Dr. Stevenson is that of Mushir Ali, a Muslim who died and reincarnated as Naresh Kumar into a Hindu family but prayed like a Muslim, without his family teaching him anything about Islam. In fact, he started praying at the age of two. At four years old, he pleaded with his father to take him to the Muslim town where he had previously lived and died, and he was able to find his past-life home and his past-life relatives and friends, naming each person correctly—even though he had never met them let alone been to this town. He also had a birth defect on the right side of his chest that reflected the trauma and rib fractures that Mushir Ali had incurred in the tractor accident that killed him.

On the other side of the coin, Dr. Stevenson investigated a case where a Hindu was killed and was reincarnated as a Muslim. The young boy retained his Hindu mind-set, even though his family taught him no such beliefs and there was no way he could have learned them on his own at that young age. And various other researchers have presented cases of Arabs who reincarnated as Jewish Israelis and vice versa, Nazis who reincarnated as Jews, and virtually every other denomination and culture reincarnating as one or the other.

Remember, as quantum physics shows us, we are all One. We are One consciousness experiencing itself as the seeming many, and this consciousness does not play favorites or hold one path to be truer than any other. Perhaps reincarnating in various cultures and religions teaches the soul tolerance. But that's not to say that we always reincarnate into a family with a different religion or culture. There are a huge number of cases that show that not only do we often come back to the same geographical area, but sometimes even reincarnate into the same family lineage. We will get into the subject of why we reincarnate and how, but for now let's continue with the evidence of its existence.

Jim Tucker, another prominent researcher who authored a book called *Life Before Life: Children's Memories of Previous Lives*,[14] focused all of this research on evidence that can be very specifically documented and used facial recognition software to *scientifically prove* that the children and their self-reported past selves in fact do share incredibly similar facial features. He also authored another book titled *Return to Life: Extraordinary Cases of Children Who Remember Past Lives*.[15] In both books, he addresses and unequivocally refutes every argument that a skeptic could raise about the subject.

OPENING OUR MINDS TO THE EVIDENCE

Now really think about this for a minute. Regardless of what you were taught when you were young or your current beliefs, there is a mountain of verifiable scientific evidence pointing to the very real fact of reincarnation that you can read for yourself; not to mention that the bulk of the verifiable evidence is coming from *children.* These are the most innocent beings of all of us, who could have no ulterior motives or agendas for making such claims. Thousands upon thousands of reports have been investigated from every walk of life and from every culture and religious upbringing. And researchers have scientifically *verified* their claims down to the last impossibly specific detail. At times, some of these details were unknown to anyone but their former selves, such as the exact place where they had buried something. Imagine the researcher's surprise when that very object was dug up and found to be precisely where the child told them it would be, despite it having been buried there many years before the child's birth in this lifetime.

At other times, knowledge of the existence of reincarnation has enabled researchers to make accurate predictions that would otherwise be impossible. In one case, a young boy claimed that he had killed himself in his previous life, and the sister of the deceased later confirmed that her brother had shot himself in the throat. The boy had shown Dr. Stevenson a birthmark on his throat, and Stevenson predicted that the boy might also have a birthmark on the top of his head, representing the exit wound from the bullet that was shot through the bottom of his throat. Upon examining the boy's head underneath his hair, a birthmark was indeed found in the exact place it was expected to be.[16]

The proof is pervasive and undeniable. Some children, for

unknown reasons, not only remember a past life but also give us so much verifiable evidence that it boggles the mind. And yet most people never hear of this. Most people are highly influenced by their own belief systems, which literally act like a giant wall around them, allowing nothing in that would disconfirm that belief system. If they happened to be born in a family that did not believe in reincarnation, then when they *do* hear about it as adults they brush it off as a false concept that some people believe in and never do any real research or investigation into the evidence. The filter of belief—belief that is most often blindly accepted in childhood and never questioned—works its magic.

And such belief, if we're not careful, can become a built-in, self-perpetuating mechanism, feeding itself by only letting us see what validates and strengthens it. All else is disregarded and even ridiculed. Being open-minded makes us discerning human beings who are empowered to know the truth without being *told* what that truth is.

THE SOUL'S JOURNEY

Now that we've explored some of the most striking evidence for reincarnation, does that mean that the concepts of heaven and hell are not real? Well, not so fast. Although there are some misconceptions regarding these subjects, the skeptics have a lot of evidence to examine too. I used to think that talk of an afterlife was merely figurative, and yet when I examined the evidence open-mindedly, I was left with no choice but to reformulate my own views.

Although the evidence is quite clear that we ultimately reincarnate into another physical form after the death of this one, does it happen instantaneously or is there some "place" where our soul goes and stays before the next physical incarnation?

In his classic books *Journey of Souls: Case Studies of Life between Lives* and *Destiny of Souls: New Case Studies of Life between Lives*, Dr. Michael Newton presents his magnificent research into what he terms "life *between* lives." [17-18] Dr. Newton openly acknowledges the fact that he was a traditional hypnotherapist who was very skeptical of the seemingly "new-age" concepts of past lives and the spirit world. And yet one experience with a client—during which the client spontaneously regressed to a previous lifetime and reported incredibly detailed facts that were later confirmed to be true—completely stunned the previously skeptical doctor.

With his worldview shaken, Dr. Newton explored such hypnotic regressions further, thereby unintentionally opening the gateway to the spirit realm (i.e., the world souls go to in between physical incarnations). After hypnotizing literally thousands of clients, he found that it didn't matter if the client was an atheist, a religiously devout person, or anything in between, once they were in the proper hypnotized state, where their conscious minds took a back seat, they were all consistent in their reports of what they saw.

Think about that. Through an advanced form of hypnosis, Dr. Newton found a way to essentially bypass their belief filters such that people with vastly differing beliefs about life and the presence (or lack thereof) of an afterlife all reported virtually the *same* things. Other highly respected therapists, such as Brian Weiss, M.D., and Delores Cannon, also present us with similar findings in their bestselling books on these subjects.[19-20] This leaves us with only one logical conclusion: How could thousands of people from all walks of life report virtually the same thing in extensive detail unless they were reporting on an actual world that exists? Only if this "spirit world" actually exists and had been visited by these people numerous times after previous deaths (before reincarnating into this current physical lifetime), would they all describe it in exacting detail in a very similar way. Indeed, as we'll see shortly, this is not merely an effect of hypnosis, as people (including children) who have near-death experiences (i.e., temporarily die and are revived back to life) provide largely the *same* descriptions as the hypnosis subjects.

And what are those descriptions? To briefly summarize, upon death of the physical body, there is absolutely no loss in consciousness whatsoever. Instead, the person experiences himself or herself as a spirit with full awareness rising out of the body and continuing to exist seamlessly without it. This is usually a very freeing and blissful experience. Some decide to linger in this state in what's called the Earth's astral realm (energetic duplicate of the physical Earth) and can even watch their own funerals and try to reach out to and console their loved ones to let them know they're OK. Eventually everyone feels drawn to go out of the Earth's plane, where they often report seeing a tunnel of light.

Let's pause here to note that while all of this seems purely spiritual, causing many scientifically minded people to be prone to dismiss it, science actually confirms such an experience completely. Many quantum physicists can now tell you that the tunnel of light is simply a wormhole that transports a spirit (i.e., energy) from this dimension into another that vibrates at a higher rate and is therefore invisible to us in this realm where we see only a small part of the electromagnetic spectrum called visible light, as we explored in the first chapter. So let's not forget all the hard science that shows how everything is energy and consciousness, and realize quite simply that the physical body is nothing more than a temporary vehicle that an aspect of this consciousness (i.e., a soul) uses to experience the illusion of physicality. And when that experience is over at the time of physical death, that consciousness is still right there, unaffected by the illusory disappearance of the seemingly physical matter.

We'll expand upon these ideas later, but for now, let's continue with what a person experiences after he or she dies, all while keeping this modern science in mind, which verifies the existence of other energetic realms that spiritually or religiously would be called the spirit world.

Upon entering the tunnel of indescribable white light, people often see someone waiting for them, who they quickly recognize to be their guide. This guide is simply an "older" soul (a more experienced soul of a higher vibrational nature) who acts as a sort of mentor as we incarnate from one lifetime to the next. Depending on how difficult this lifetime has been (involving emotional and/or physical trauma), our soul may be taken for energy cleansing and restoration. After that, there is what's referred to as a life review, in which the soul steps into holographic, three-dimensional scenes from his or her life just lived and re-experiences every pain (and joy) that he or she caused others in that life, feeling it directly from the others' point of view. The religious references to judgment, which are often misinterpreted to be wrathful and carried out on us by an external judge, are seen here to be nothing more than the re-experiencing of every hurt we caused other beings so that we can learn to be more loving and kind. I'll return more to this and the whole purpose of reincarnation in later chapters, where I'll explore it in great detail on a more grand, cosmic level. For now, let's continue on with what is usually reported to happen next.

After the energy cleansing and life reviews, we are taken to reunite with the souls of our loved ones. If we have always assumed physical death to be the ultimate end, then we might take comfort in knowing that all the empirical evidence from hypnosis subjects, as well as near-death experiences, points to the fact that not only do we still exist after death but also reunite with those we thought we had lost. Once again, this is completely supported from the new scientific standpoint that tells us that not only is physical matter an illusion altogether (so that its seeming death would not really mean anything) but also that energy can never be destroyed—it can only change form (remember Einstein's equation, $E=mc^2$).

SOUL GROUPS

It is also notable that those closest to us while we are on Earth seem to make up what is called a "soul group" in the spirit world or the life-between-lives world.[17] Soul groups can include anywhere from a few to around 25 souls, who are usually of similar vibrational energy levels (i.e., similar spiritual progress) and will reincarnate with one another one lifetime after the next, playing different roles to learn new lessons in each life. For instance, in one life you could be the son of one of the souls in your soul group, in the next, that soul could be your son; in another, you may be sisters (souls don't have a physical sex and will regularly incarnate in physical bodies of both sexes), and in yet another, best friends or lovers. There are also other soul groups that are close to yours and with whom you often interact in various roles during these physical lifetimes. All the hypnosis subjects alike, regardless of race, culture, religion, or other beliefs, reported the existence of soul groups. It seems to be the standard way things operate.

Carrying on, while the landscape of the spirit realm is purely nonphysical and energetic, it "looks" physical to the souls that inhabit it. Remember, scientifically speaking, physicality is nothing more than slower vibrating energy. The faster the energy is vibrating, the less "physical" it will seem to be. But because we can only perceive that which is of the same vibrational frequency range as us, this means that although we wouldn't be able to see the spirit realm with our physical eyes, we would see it as seemingly solid when we experience it as souls because we would be of the same vibrational frequency as it while in that state of being.

Therefore, people often report seeing breathtaking views, such as "heavenly" landscapes and even buildings and structures that are reminiscent of things we see on earth—just much more magnificent and wondrous. Also, while our loved ones will often initially appear to us in the form of who they were in the most recent lifetime (to give us comfort during our transition), all souls appear simply as energy with a distinct color. The colors denote their level of spiritual advancement, or scientifically speaking, their vibrational frequency. Science shows us that each color has a different frequency or rate of vibration associated with it, and the more advanced a soul is in spiritual terms, the higher its frequency of energy will be.

OUR TIME IN THE SPIRIT REALM

We must understand that time doesn't exist in the spirit realm in the same way as it does on the physical plane. While it's beyond the scope of this book to go into the fascinating science of time, quantum physicists have discovered that it is not linear at all. Time, like matter, is merely an illusion, and in fact, it is three-dimensional/ holographic instead of linear.[21] This means that through either consciousness or advanced technology, it is possible to go to any "space" *in time*, whether seemingly forward or backward, as it's not at all a straight line like we experience it to be.

Practically speaking, this means that we often spend what would seem to be hundreds of years in the spirit realm in between lifetimes, but we can then choose to incarnate into a physical body only nine months after our last body died. This lack of understanding of the structure of time is what has created a misperception among some believers in reincarnation, in which they think that a soul that has just experienced physical body death in one lifetime is instantly transferred into a new body inside a mother who has just become pregnant, as they know of numerous cases of children who remembered their past lives and were born only nine months after their previous deaths. But with the correct view of the illusory nature of time, it can be understood that there could have been a "long" interval spent in the higher vibrational spirit realm before the reincarnation only nine months later.

In terms of what we do during all that time spent in between physical lifetimes, the thousands of hypnosis subjects reported similar things, such as souls attending spiritual classrooms of sorts, taking part in various forms of recreation, learning from advanced souls about how to work with energy, and many other things. By all accounts, though, the one common element of the spirit realm is its heavenly nature. That is, all the souls exist in a world of harmony, kindness, patience, and absolute love. Even if a soul in your group or another one has harmed you in the physical life you just lived, there is no resentment or ill will present on either side. It is fundamentally understood that physical life is nothing more than a theater of sorts in which we play out varying roles and learn from our mistakes and transgressions so that we can become more loving and advance spiritually. And this brings us directly back to Shakespeare's famous quote, which can now be seen for the truly perceptive and fundamentally truth-revealing statement it is: "All the world's a stage... and all the men and women merely players." Indeed, far from being metaphor, as many have believed it to be, in light of the empirical evidence from thousands upon thousands of people, it seems to be an accurate depiction of reality.

And so at some point, we (with the help of our guide) decide that it's time again for another physical incarnation. Here we are taken to a life selection place where we are given the choice of one of several bodies and lives that we can choose to live. We are given the opportunity to see the major events that will occur that will test us in each of the potential lives while keeping enough hidden so as not to dissuade us from difficult but potentially beneficial lives from the spiritual sense.

Again, remember what quantum physics tells us about the nature of time. It is possible to choose among various "future" lifetimes and to see the major events in each one because time is an illusion. It is much more accurate to think of it as a three-dimensional space than as a line that runs only forward. As a three-dimensional space, we can choose any coordinate we want and experience it, whether it would be called the past or the future from our current perspective. It's important to keep all the real science in mind and not to fall into the trap of relegating all this to mere fantasy or speculation. Not only are we getting the data from thousands of people who are in a state of hypnosis and therefore accessing unconscious memories but also all of them are saying the same thing regardless of their backgrounds and beliefs. This point cannot be overstated.

THE CLASSROOM OF LIFE

And so what's the purpose of incarnating again, and on what basis are we given the new physical bodies from which to choose? The purpose is simply to have the opportunity to learn the lessons that we failed to learn in all of our previous lifetimes so far. And the lessons center on nothing more than love, kindness, forgiveness, and compassion. This is what's at the heart of all the religious and spiritual messages we have received throughout history, and this is the ultimate purpose of reincarnation: to give us many chances or opportunities to get it right. It would be difficult to evolve and perfect the soul if we had only one life in which to try. We are given many lifetimes so that we have a chance to learn from our mistakes and learn the only appropriate reaction to any circumstance that befalls us on earth: unconditional love.

As such, the life that we choose will by definition include certain difficult trials and tribulations to induce the lessons we failed to learn in previous lifetimes. For instance, if we were arrogant and unkind in a previous life, then we may choose a life where we will be forced to learn humility by being born poor or with a physical disability. So instead of looking at such a state as being given less by God, whereas others seem to have been favored, it can be correctly understood that we all end up going through all possible conditions, such that it is pointless to complain about poor circumstances or feel overly joyful about good ones. Looked at from our evidence-based perspective, we can see that, whatever our circumstances, they were *chosen by us* from the soul level in order for us to learn lessons and progress spiritually. Similarly, those with the concept that reincarnating as a poor or disabled person means that we are being punished by a supreme being for what we did in our previous lifetime fail to realize that it is we ourselves who choose the difficult life in order to learn and grow.

Think how much more sense life makes and how much easier it is to accept things when looked at from this perspective. We are not victims of some greater force outside us. We are not "unlucky." We do not get "punished" for our transgressions. We need not cry out "God, why me?" when unexpected or unwanted things occur. We need only to understand that we, with the help of more evolved beings, set it all up this way for a very specific purpose. And while a veil of forgetfulness is placed on our minds when we reincarnate so that we can have the best chance of learning these lessons without previous life memories interfering, keeping this ultimate reality in the back of our mind can be very helpful and prove to be a self-empowered way to live life. Even that minority of children who remember their past lives can feel a great sense of relief by understanding that everything has been chosen by them on a soul level. Everything has a purpose.

SCIENTIFIC PROOF OF HEAVEN

If you were thinking that we only have hypnosis subjects to help us map out spiritual reality, you're in for more fascinating discoveries. The near-death experience (or NDE) is a phenomenon that provides a wealth of evidence to support Dr.

Newton's research, and that of other prominent hypnotherapists such as Brian Weiss, and Delores Cannon.[19-20]

The term "near-death experience" was coined by Dr. Raymond Moody in his fascinating book *Life After Life*.[22] According to the definition given by the International Association for Near Death Studies, an NDE is an experience that occurs with some people who have a near-death episode, whereby the person is pronounced clinically dead, is very close to death, or is in a situation where death is quite likely or even expected.[23] Many NDErs have stated that the term *near death* is incorrect because what they experienced was being *in death* and not just near it (and indeed many are clinically pronounced dead by doctors).

Literally millions of people around the world have reported NDEs—including many notable figures such as Carl Jung and George Lucas—so we have a large base of empirical data from which to draw. The list of cases includes a vast number of NDEs reported by children, who, again, state what they see and experience in the most innocent and unbiased of ways. The vast majority of the experiences involve mostly feelings of immense love, joy, peace, and bliss. Only a relatively small number of people report negative NDEs that involve fearful situations and feelings. In all cases, people report the experience to be hyper-real, even more real than earthly life. And the most interesting fact from these millions of personal accounts is that we find very similar correlations to the reports of the hypnosis subjects: they have an out-of-body experience whereby they are completely conscious despite not experiencing that consciousness within their body (sometimes even looking down on the physical body), seeing a tunnel of light (i.e., a wormhole to another dimension), encountering deceased loved ones after going through the tunnel, meeting with very loving spiritual beings, a life review, incredibly beautiful landscapes, and an awesome sense of knowledge and life purpose.

Despite the obvious transformational results that such experiences usually have on people, and despite the undeniable physical proof of being out of body while completely unconscious or even clinically dead (such as being able to tell the doctors, nurses, and relatives very specific details of what they were talking about, sometimes even if those people weren't in the room with the clinically dead person, or seeing future events with spiritual guides and then watching those events come to pass with exact precision later in life), most doctors remain skeptical and claim that NDEs are hallucinations caused by the brain in its temporary traumatic state near death. However, the ultimate proof that these are *not* hallucinations came from Dr. Eben Alexander, who documented his very rare NDE in his incredible book *Proof of Heaven: A Neurosurgeon's Journey into the Afterlife.*[24]

Prior to his own NDE, Dr. Alexander was a neurosurgeon who was the ultimate skeptic. He had had many patients who claimed to have experienced profound NDEs, but he always dismissed them as hallucinations. He was very quickly forced to change his views, however, when he contracted a rare virus and went into a coma for seven days. What is interesting about this occurrence, unlike any other, is that he contracted a brain virus that completely shut down his brain. Under such a situation, with the brain 100 percent inoperative, it would be impossible for it to even create hallucinations. So if it were true that the brain creates consciousness, as so many neurosurgeons believe, then it would be a literal impossibility for Dr. Alexander to experience *anything* whatsoever. His brain could not have produced thought or emotion, and indeed, all electrical brain activity that was monitored throughout his weeklong coma showed absolutely nothing. Yet he wasn't experiencing "nothing."

Far from feeling or seeing nothing, Dr. Alexander had the most profound encounter. He visited the realm of the afterlife and had incredible experiences—all while his brain was completely shut down. He could not have dreamed it or imagined it because his brain was uniquely inoperative from the rare virus. Because this scientifically rules out any hallucination or "made-up" experience or imagination whatsoever, the only scientific conclusion possible is that Dr. Alexander was in an out-of-body state, as pure consciousness, and the realm he spoke of and what he saw was all 100 percent *real*.

His account is completely fascinating and scientifically *revolutionary* given the way it occurred. It unequivocally proved that not only do we never lose consciousness but also that awareness can take many unique forms (he reported being simply a point of awareness at various times with no self-concept or identity, which confirms the science we explored earlier that showed *everything* is aware). It also points to the existence of a very real realm that is, to describe it most directly, heavenly.

What makes Dr. Alexander's story most interesting is that while it did scientifically confirm the experiences of other NDErs, as well as the hypnosis subjects of researchers like Dr. Newton, it seemed to go beyond the life-between-lives realm to an actual heavenly realm of a most beautiful and profound nature, giving us a peek into the wondrous realms that exist beyond physical life.

BEYOND HUMAN EXISTENCE

Could these realms be where we're headed as we evolve our soul through the cyclical earthly incarnations? Before we explore this fascinating subject and answer the ultimate question of why are we here, we must answer another question most of us have asked: Are we alone in the universe?

Indeed, this question is of utmost importance and directly related to everything we've been exploring so far. If we are not the only (or even the most) intelligent or advanced life form in the universe, then what would that mean? Where would that leave us in terms of our purpose as humans? What would it mean about the grand design of the whole universe and life itself, including the physical and various nonphysical realms we've been exploring in this chapter?

I personally believe that we can only come to a truly full understanding of the universe and the purpose of life if we explore the possibility that we are a part of a much larger structure that goes farther than not only physical life as we've been exploring so far but also humanity as a whole.

And as you're about to see, we don't need to theorize to come up with conclusions about life outside this planet. On this subject matter, the proof is literally everywhere. And if you haven't explored this subject in detail before, then you're in for a big, reality-changing surprise. Later, in Chapter 6, we'll take all of that information and tie it into everything we've learned so far to arrive at a detailed understanding of the hidden structure of existence and our place in it all.

CHAPTER 5

WE ARE
NOT ALONE

"Yes there have been crashed craft, and
bodies recovered. We are not alone in the universe;
they have been coming here for a long time."

– DR. EDGAR MITCHELL

Perhaps the greatest discovery humanity could make would be to find out that we are not alone and there is indeed extraterrestrial life. That would arguably cause the biggest reformulation of our belief systems about life and the universe. But what if this discovery has already been made, but is being suppressed for various purposes by governments around the world?

In this chapter, we'll explore the evidence of our true cosmic history and current state of affairs. All we need to do is to put judgment aside and look at that evidence with an open mind, and we'll see the truth emerge on its own and fit in wonderfully with everything we've been discovering so far.

To help with that, ask yourself: "How do I *know* that the history of Earth and humanity is true?" You were born not too long ago, relatively speaking, and you were quickly taught what reality is and how the world operates. But from the first few chapters in this book alone, you've already seen that much of what we're taught is simply not a true depiction of reality. And so how do we know it's not also the case with regard to the history of this planet and our species? How do we know that nearly all of it isn't false information that has been merely circulated and written about within the last few hundred years to hide a history very different from what has taken place (and which continues to this day)?

What you're about to see is a grand puzzle coming together piece by piece, and central to this puzzle is the existence and involvement of a multitude of civilizations from beyond our planet. Not only are we not alone but also our "visitors" have been with us for millennia. The proof is all around us to see if we think with an open mind and dare to remove the blindfold that's been placed over our eyes.

EARTH IS NOT THE ONLY ONE

Scientists have recently confirmed that there are likely 20 *billion* earthlike planets in our galaxy alone. [25] And there are a couple hundred billion observable galaxies. That's *billion* with a B. And given that many of these planets are older than Earth, it is very reasonable to expect that many would have hosted life earlier than it. This means that they could have had a few million to a couple *billion* more years than us to evolve technologically. In fact, if we know that Earth is 4.5 billion years old, and there happens to be an earthlike planet that is merely 4.501 billion years old, then the planet and any civilization on it would have had an entire million years more to evolve. If we've evolved this fast in just a few

70

thousand years, then what would a million extra years of evolution do? Can you imagine where such a civilization would be? Now how about one that is a *billion years* older?

If we think back to the first two chapters, which detailed what quantum physicists now understand about the universe, we'll remember that not only is matter fundamentally an illusion but so is *time and space*. For any advanced civilization that discovered this, it would mean the ability to travel seemingly unimaginable distances in extremely short periods of time, using technology that could warp time and space at a quantum level. For me, all this clearly points to the extremely high probability not only for life outside Earth but also for extremely advanced life that can easily travel here. And as we look at the mounds of real evidence, we'll see that this is precisely what has occurred.

A MONUMENT LIKE NO OTHER

Conventional researchers and scientists would have us believe that the Great Pyramid of Giza in Egypt was a tomb built for the pharaohs with the use of slaves around 2,560 BC. Because most people haven't taken the time to research this monument in any in-depth manner, this theory about its origin is taken as fact and left at that. But a few unorthodox researchers have bravely dared to question conventional history and wisdom, and they have given us a very different picture of the Great Pyramid and who its builders likely were.

Let's start with this fascinating summary by researcher David Pratt:

"The Pyramid is an unrivaled feat of engineering and craftsmanship. It is aligned with the four cardinal points more accurately than any

contemporary structure, including the Meridian Building at Greenwich Observatory in London. The 350-foot-long descending passage is so straight that it deviates from a central axis by less than a quarter of an inch from side to side and only one-tenth of an inch up and down—comparable with the best laser-controlled drilling being done today. The casing stones, some of which weighed over 16 tons, are so perfectly shaped and squared that the mortar-filled joint between them is just one-fiftieth of an inch—the thickness of a human nail. Egyptologist Sir Flinders Petrie described such phenomenal precision as "the finest opticians' work. Work of this caliber is beyond the capabilities of modern technology." The casing stones show no tool marks and the corners are not even slightly chipped. The granite coffer in the King's Chamber is cut out of a solid block of hard red granite—so precisely that its external volume is exactly twice its internal volume. Engineer and master craftsman Christopher Dunn rejects the theory that it could have been cut and hollowed using bronze saws set with diamond cutting points, because when pressure was applied, the diamonds would have worked their way into the much softer copper, leaving the granite virtually unscathed. In his opinion, the evidence shows that the Egyptians would have to have possessed ultra-modern tools, including tubular drills that could cut granite 500 times faster than modern drills. But that is not all. The Great Pyramid embodies an advanced knowledge of geometry, geodesy (the science of earth measurement), and astronomy."[26]

Let's take a moment to really think about this and weigh the implications instead of simply dismissing it as a group of interesting facts and moving on. These scientists and engineers are stating outright that to build this great monument with such unimaginable precision is *beyond the capabilities of modern technology.* Not just slightly beyond but, as in the case of the drilling, 500 times more advanced! Even today, thousands of years after the Great Pyramid was built, we are still very far away from being able to create a comparable structure using the most modern available technology.

In fact, in the 1970's a Japanese team funded by Nissan tried to duplicate the Great Pyramid of Giza at only one-quarter scale by employing modern technology, and they failed miserably.[27] They simply couldn't do it, even when using laser-controlled drilling. This showed that the most advanced laser technology we have cannot achieve the same precision by which the pyramid was built. And yet we're to accept the theory that it was built by slaves using crude tools? You don't have to be "open-minded" to think that an advanced non-terrestrial civilization built the Great Pyramid.

But this is just the start of it. Take a look at the following mind-bending facts:[28]

- The pyramid has around 2.3 million stone blocks that weigh up to 30 tons each. *(Even today's largest cranes would break when trying to lift just one of these mammoth stones, and yet 2.3 million of them were placed with perfect precision and exact mathematical relationships.)*

- The outer layer was made of 144,000 highly polished casing stones, around 100 inches (254cm) wide and each weighing about 15 tons—all flat to an accuracy of 0.001 inch (0.00254cm). *(Today's most advanced technology would have a difficult time polishing any stone to this kind of astonishing accuracy. And there are 144,000 of them.)*

- The mortar used is of an unknown origin. Scientists have analyzed it and determined its chemical composition (which is stronger than the stone itself), but have been unable to reproduce it. *(Try wrapping your mind around this one.)*

- The pyramid is the most precisely aligned structure on Earth, facing true north with only 3/60th degree of error. *(Even now, it is still aligned with the four cardinal points more accurately than any other modern structure on Earth, including the Meridian Building at Greenwich Observatory in London, which is humanity's current pinnacle of precision.)*

- The base length of the Great Pyramid multiplied by 43,200 is equal to the equatorial circumference of Earth, with better than one percent accuracy. The height times this exact same number of 43,200 is equal to the Earth's polar radius, accurate to 0.2 percent. *(Whoever built it knew the Earth wasn't a perfect sphere because there were different measures for the equatorial and polar circumferences.)*

- The centers of the four sides are indented with an incredible degree of precision. This indentation can only be seen from the air under precise lighting conditions. *(Today's laser instruments now show that this perfect concavity of its sides precisely duplicates the curvature of the Earth.)*

While this information is unbelievable, even more stunning is that it only scratches the surface. The pyramid not only shows unexplainable precision and understanding of the Earth's every measurement in terms of mass, radius, and curvature with impeccable accuracy but also reveals that exact astronomical measurements were also known, some of which we have only been recently able to measure with our own advanced technology.

In light of all of this incredible information, are we really expected to believe that the Egyptians built the pyramids? That a civilization much less technologically advanced than our own built a monument that is so advanced in every possible way that we can't even come close to replicating something a quarter of its size?

Now let me offer a different hypothesis. Whoever built the Great Pyramid was clearly not from here. They had vastly advanced knowledge of Earth and space as well as a very superior understanding of mathematics, technology, and building techniques that are light years ahead of ours.

So do we have other pieces of historical evidence that point to the same conclusion? Indeed we do, and more than you might imagine.

ANCIENT ART REVEALS AN ANCIENT SECRET

If extraterrestrials have been visiting the Earth for a long time, as *Apollo 14* astronaut Edgar Mitchell claims, then there should be more historical evidence of their visits than just one out-of-this-world monument like the Great Pyramid. And in fact, there are many more monuments around the world that still leave scientists absolutely baffled.

One such mystifying monument is the huge-scale geoglyphs in the desert of Peru, known as the Nazca Lines.[29] These ancient lines range from geometric patterns to drawings of animal and human forms. The baffling thing is that they are so gigantic that they can only be fully seen from high in the air. But how could they have been completed so long before humans could fly to map out such massive designs with such unerring precision?

Another monument that has left researchers utterly

mystified is the ruins of Baalbek in Lebanon. More specifically, what they discovered there was a feat of engineering that is as yet unexplained. Other than the Podium, which was built with some of the largest stone blocks ever cut, we find the world's largest crafted stone block, weighing a mind-boggling 1,000 tons.[30] To put that in perspective, that's almost as much as three Boeing 747 aircrafts. And if today's largest cranes would break trying to lift one 30-ton stone (such as the ones the Great Pyramid was built with), how could primitive people have possibly crafted and lifted one weighing 30 times that much? Once again, it doesn't require too much of an open mind to ponder the very logical likelihood that it wasn't done by humans at all.

But despite such truly mystifying monuments (and many more around the world that scientists still can't explain), most people quickly assume that there is no evidence because that's what they've been told by mainstream media and science, who often marginalize the subject of "aliens" and make it a fringe topic that is worthy only of derision and condescending jokes.

That alone should raise a flag for you because if you know anything, then you know that the propaganda machine that we call modern media can't be trusted. For them to go so far out of their way to belittle a subject should be a big clue that they know it's actually true and have a vested interest in keeping it suppressed. (Think big corporations who would go out of business overnight, and elites who would lose their power, if the truth of highly advanced extraterrestrial technology were revealed.)

But you don't simply have to theorize about this because not only do we have countless monuments of impossibly advanced engineering around the world, but the historical evidence is also all around us in the form of ancient art. As it turns out, nearly every ancient civilization that we know of has depicted contact with extraterrestrials in their art. Most historians will say that these are simply the drawings of cavemen and represent their imaginations, but as you look at the art, you'll see the absolute absurdity of this claim.

Why? Because if it were just the imagination and myths of ancient tribes that were drawn in caves and carved in metals, then what are the odds that the drawings would look very similar, even though the tribes existed thousands of miles and even thousands of years apart? Coincidence?

Every tribe just happened to imagine an object that we now call a "flying saucer" and they all visualized it looking the same way, and they were all so taken by their imaginations that they spent untold amounts of time carving and painting detailed accounts of it? I'll let you be the judge of the likelihood of that as you look at a small selection of the art.

First, we have a cave painting found in France, dating to around 13,000 BC shown in figure 5.1 below, which depicts the typical image of a flying saucer or spaceship that we're all accustomed to. And yet it was painted some 15,000 years ago.

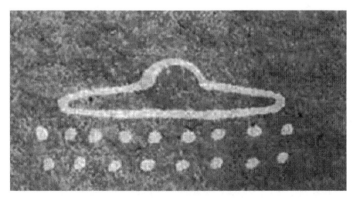

Figure 5.1 15,000-year-old cave painting in
France, seeming to depict a spaceship

Then there's this cave painting shown in figure 5.2, dating to 10,000 BC, from Val Camonica, Italy, which seems to depict two beings in protective "space" suits.

Figure 5.2 Italian cave painting showing two beings wearing "space" suits

Next, in figure 5.3, we see a cave drawing from Tassili n'Ajjer in the Sahara Desert in North Africa, dating to 6,000 BC. Once again, we see the prototypical spaceship in the distance in the top right, with some sort of alien being front and center.

Figure 5.3 African cave drawing depicting a flying saucer and alien being

Most strikingly, we have the ancient artwork of the Mayans. The Mexican government recently released an archeological find that had been kept secret for about 80 years. Figure 5.4 depicts this incredible finding that seems to be portraying extraterrestrial contact. Once again, you can see the typical flying saucers, yet incredibly, this image actually shows a close-up view of what's in the spaceship. As you can see in the top center, an extraterrestrial being is clearly depicted manning the craft.

Figure 5.4 Mayan art depicting an extraterrestrial being manning a spacecraft

Figure 5.5 shows more Mayan artwork, this one being perhaps the clearest picture of a spaceship we've seen yet, complete with the light beam coming down and a being standing beneath it.

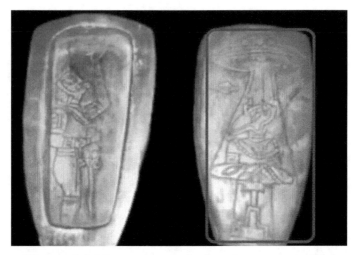

Figure 5.5 Mayan artwork showing a spaceship
beaming light down onto a being

So we have different tribes and civilizations, from completely different eras, all depicting similar things in their ancient art. Imagination? Coincidence? I hardly think so.

And to corroborate the evidence in the Mayan art, one of the highest ranking government officials in Mexico, Luis Augusto Garcia Rosado, has gone on record stating that the government has also found aircraft "landing pads" in the jungle that are 3,000 years old that are kept quarantined.[31]

But it doesn't end with the ancient civilizations. Artistic evidence from more recent history abounds, and it is truly remarkable. Take a look at the painting depicted in figure 5.6, which is believed to have been painted by Domenico Ghirlandaio around the 15th century. Mother Mary is looking downward, and in the background to her right, you can clearly see what looks to be some sort of spaceship flying above and a man looking up at it. The flying saucer is shining with lights and looks very similar to the ancient art we've just seen.

Figure 5.6 15th-century painting of Mother Mary
with a flying saucer in the background

Now if spaceships were not regularly seen in those times, then why would this artist depict it so blatantly in his work? Wouldn't that diminish the seriousness of the piece and open it up to ridicule at the time, unless this was a known and relatively normal occurrence? And if you investigate the subject further, you'll find that he was only one of many artists who depicted them, with others such as Carlo Crivelli (*The Annunciation with Saint Emidius, 1486*) and Arendt de Gelder (*Baptism of Jesus*, 1710) prominently featuring them in their art as well.

Once again, how could all of these works look so similar unless they were depicting something from reality that everyone was simply observing? What are the odds that every culture across history has "imagined" spaceships and that they've imagined them to look the same way?

Although this artistic proof is compelling and clear, when it is coupled with the following remarkable evidence it becomes utterly convincing.

THE DOGON TRIBE AND THE BEINGS FROM THE STARS

The Dogon people live in the Hombori Mountains near Timbuktu. They are an ancient tribe whose history is believed to date back to around 3,000 BC. Dogon mythology is complex and at first sounds like a bunch of stories told by an uncivilized tribe. Since ancient times, until now, they talk about amphibious beings that came to Earth from the Sirius star system for the benefit of mankind. These beings supposedly served as guides and teachers and are greatly revered by the Dogon.

The ancient Dogon Tribe has long described the exact location and orbit of the stars from which their visitors supposedly came, and this information is at the focal point of their ancient mythology. But as astronomers have recently discovered, mythology may not be the right word for it. As it turns out, the star that the Dogon talked about and gave exact coordinates for (even though it is not visible to the naked eye) was photographed through advanced telescopes in 1970. It is so difficult to observe that earlier telescopes couldn't even detect it. And yet, when it was detected, it was exactly where the Dogon Tribe claimed it would be. This star is now known as Sirius B.

The Dogon claimed that it is a very heavy, small, white star, and sure enough, astronomers have confirmed that it is indeed a white dwarf, which is a very heavy, small, white star. Their so-called mythology also claimed that the star where their space visitors came from has an elliptical orbit, with another star at one focus of the ellipse, and that the orbital period is 50 years. When our technology was sufficiently advanced enough to photograph and measure these distant invisible stars, it was found that indeed there is another star located precisely where the Dogon said it would be (this is now called Sirius A) and that the orbital period is indeed 50 years.

As if that weren't enough, their "mythology" also includes Saturn's rings and Jupiter's four moons, and they have long known that Earth and the other planets orbit the sun, well before it was officially "discovered" by Copernicus a few hundred years ago.[32]

As logical, educated human beings, how do we explain how an "uncivilized" ancient tribe could have such exact knowledge of the cosmos, which has only recently been discovered by modern science with all of our advanced technology? The conclusion is inescapable. The Dogon, exactly as they claim, received the knowledge by extraterrestrials from the Sirius star cluster. While this may sound impossible, there is no other sound conclusion given the literal impossibility of them having this kind of precise cosmic information for thousands of years.

And when coupled with the ancient art across ages and civilizations, as well as the mind-boggling technological wonder that is the Great Pyramid (and many others throughout the world such as the Nazca lines, Baalbek, Stonehenge, and the Easter Island heads), that conclusion becomes all the more inescapable. We are not alone. And as Apollo 14 astronaut Edgar Mitchell has stated, "they" have been coming here for a very long time.

But does that mean this is all ancient history? Or are they *still* coming here? As you're about to see, the evidence is also everywhere that they are still visiting all the time.

BEYOND PAINTINGS: PROOF IN PICTURES

The following is a small sample of photographs from the 1940's and 50's. Please note that recently, with the advent of Photoshop, many alleged UFO pictures are not authentic. However, many of the earlier photographs were taken and distributed publicly before such software was available to change the images, which is why I present the earlier photographs. Also, many of the earlier photographs have been studied by scientists in laboratories and *officially authenticated* by several independent photographic experts, who came to the unequivocal conclusion that no photo tampering whatsoever has been done. Try to keep that important fact in mind, as you look at the following photographs.

Figure 5.7 Outer Hebrides,
Scotland, 1947

Czaplinek, Poland 1947, Photographer unknown

Figure 5.8 Czaplinek, Poland, 1947

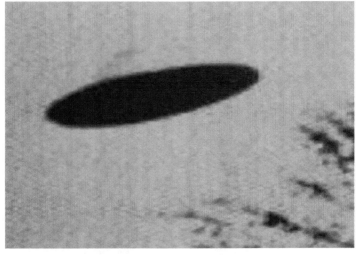

Figure 5.9 Illinois, USA, 1950

Figure 5.10 Oregon, USA, 1950

Passiac, New Jersey, 1952

Figure 5.11 Passiac, New Jersey, 1952

Now that you've seen a small sample of this photographic evidence (there are thousands more from around the world), there's something that I'm sure you noticed. And that's that the vast majority of these spaceships look *exactly* like the ones depicted in historical art. So there we have our modern-day picture proof of what these old civilizations must have been witnessing firsthand and recording on the walls of their caves, on their metals, and in their paintings and tapestries. In my view it's clear that it's not merely coincidence that they all drew similar objects in the sky despite being separated by incredible geographic and temporal distances. They were simply reporting what they saw.

Proof in the Fields: The Crop Circle Phenomenon

Our contemporary form of evidence doesn't come just from pictures. We also have undeniable evidence from unexplained phenomena in the fields of farmers, called "crop circles," and you can see why when you look at the pictures. Basically, the crops form unexplainable patterns, whereby the stalks of the plants are flattened yet stay alive, forming a contrast with the remaining standing stalks, which creates the pattern. Over 5,000 of these crop circles have been found in more than 30 countries, most commonly in the UK.

The thing that is just as impressive as the unimaginably complex symbols and mathematical riddles embedded in the massive crop circles (which some researchers have dedicated their careers to understanding) is how fast they appear. One day the farmer will have a normal field, and the next morning it will show massive and very elaborate symbols and artwork. There are also reports of people flying over a field in a small plane, and then only 15 minutes later flying back over it to see a gigantic and highly complex crop circle there that wasn't present minutes earlier. It's clear that humans do not have the ability to create such elaborate patterns, especially not in such a short period of time and especially while never—*ever*—being detected.

But of course, if you ask mainstream scientists, they often claim that they're all the work of humans. Now, as with anything else, you will get some hoaxes and fakes. So the mainstream scientists, who are baffled or even threatened by the real phenomenon, will use the few hoaxes to discredit all crop circles and claim that they are all the work of humans. But one thing they never tell you is that all the fakes are of obviously much lower quality than the unexplained originals, lacking the precision and complexity of the real thing. And they also fail to address the question of how such an incredibly complex and highly precise massive pattern can appear in a matter of hours, or even minutes at times. Moreover, they completely ignore the findings of non-mainstream (i.e., non-corporate-controlled) scientists.

Before we get to such findings, take a look at a small sample of some crop circles photographed in various fields in the UK (where these phenomena occur with the highest frequency).

Figure 5.12 Windmill Hill, Sussex, UK

Figure 5.13 Sugar Hill, Dorset, UK

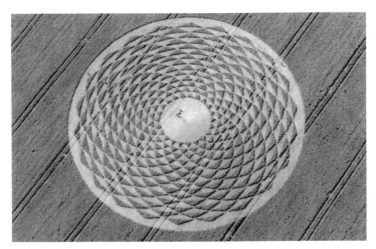

Figure 5.14 Cherhill, Wiltshire, UK

Figure 5.15 Wiltshire, UK

As you can see, the precision and complexity of the crop circles is utterly remarkable. Look at a few in detail and you quickly realize that claiming that humans are creating these (in a matter of hours and sometimes even minutes) is illogical. Just the visual proof and the knowledge of how quickly they are accomplished is enough evidence to show that something out of the ordinary is taking place here. But there is also plenty of scientific evidence to support the visual proof.

THE STRANGE SCIENCE OF CROP CIRCLES

In 1991, Michael Chorost and Marshall Dudley, two US nuclear physicists, conducted numerous tests on crop circles. The first thing they were impressed by was the perfection in the swirling of the plants. Chorost, initially a skeptic, commented that they were "technical and artistic masterpieces." But after subjecting seeds and soil samples to rigorous lab analysis, they discovered that the soil contained at least four short-lived radioactive isotopes not known to be produced in nature. They also stated that "the isotopes are not known to be emissions from atomic tests, nuclear power plants, or Chernobyl."

Basically, the soil within the crop formations was two to three times as radioactive as soil from outside it. The scientists stated, "We carefully considered a variety of other mundane causes: natural radionuclides, cosmogenic radionuclides, sample jar contamination, airport X-ray detectors, thermal neutron activators, and contamination with hospital waste by hoaxers. None of them held up as valid sources."[33]

They also asked molecular biologist Kevin Folta to analyze DNA samples from the plants in the crop circles and found that they were considerably affected by radiation.[34] Another scientist, Dr. Levengood, independently found consistent anomalies in plants from crop circles around the world, including node swelling, cell wall pit enhancement, polyembryony, increased seed germination rates, and variations in oxidation and reduction characteristics.[35] This suggests that the plants affected have been subjected to a short burst of rapid heating and cooling.

But perhaps the most interesting part is that the crop circles have not been found to pose any threat to the health of people who step inside them (except for very short-term dizziness and nausea). To date, no long-term health risks have been reported by the hundreds of thousands of visitors to the fields, despite the evident radiation. This suggests that whatever this form of radiation is, it's not the one we're normally used to on Earth.

Other scientists have also found that the electromagnetic field over the crop circle is often mysteriously electrostatically charged and that there are strange magnetic particles on the crops.

By contrast, the confirmed hoaxed crop circles, which again are clearly inferior in design, do not show the same radiation or electromagnetic phenomena. Hoax theorists seem to disregard these obvious points, and they also don't add up all the other clear evidence we've been discussing, which offers a much more coherent picture of what's actually going on.

But if everything we've explored so far wasn't enough evidence of extraterrestrial presence on Earth, we also have remarkable eyewitness accounts and whistleblower testimony from the highest levels of government and military confirming this evidence.

WHISTLEBLOWERS CONFIRM THE TRUTH

Let's start with former air force pilot and astronaut Gordon Cooper. Cooper has gone on record to talk about the 1951 UFO incident that he and other air force pilots witnessed. While flying their jets, the pilots saw literally hundreds of massive UFOs flying in formation at an extremely high altitude, which the jets couldn't get anywhere near. The vast armada of UFOs stayed visible for a day and a half. The pilots filed an official report and sent it to the government, only to have it ignored.[35]

Six years later, in 1957, Colonel Cooper had another UFO encounter, while supervising flight-testing at Edwards Air Force Base in California. His military camera crew was filming at the base when a saucer-shaped craft approached and actually landed nearby. They began filming it but when they got very close, it retracted its landing gear, hovered, and then took off at an incredible rate of speed. The crew, who immediately showed the footage to Cooper, captured all this on camera. After developing and viewing the film, he went through all the proper regulations of reporting it and sending it to Washington, and to his surprise, no one has ever seen it since.

But the interesting thing is that in both the 1951 and 1957 incidents, the flying saucers that Cooper and the other pilots saw looked extremely similar to the ones we've seen in the historical art and modern pictures. In an interview with journalist Yolanda Gaskins, Cooper explains the scientific reason behind this shape, stating that the saucer is very aerodynamic and has the ability to go through the atmosphere at tremendous rates of speed without making shockwaves (and therefore being able to remain silent). This would explain why we see the same shapes depicted throughout history. The ancient civilizations and artists of the past were not all coincidentally imagining similar shaped objects flying in the sky. More logically, they were depicting real events of highly advanced flying crafts.

And remember, this is a former US Air Force pilot and astronaut with many colleagues that witnessed the same things. He not only has no reason to make things up but also has much to lose if he were to do so. If you had the credibility and respect of an air force pilot and astronaut, then you would not likely risk it by stating such things unless they were 100 percent real and you absolutely knew the truth.

Now let's go higher up the ranks and discover the testimony of someone who would have even more to lose in terms of respect and public image by talking about such seemingly "fringe" subjects that are often ridiculed by the media and many mainstream scientists.

In 2013, Paul Hellyer, the former defense minister of Canada, testified in front of former members of the US Congress in a citizen hearing on UFO disclosure.

During that hearing he unequivocally stated: "UFOs are as real as the airplanes over our heads." He also incredibly testified that government reports have been issued, confirming that at least four extraterrestrial species have been visiting the Earth for thousands of years.[36] The fact that they've been visiting for thousands of years corroborates astronaut Edgar Mitchell's claims, as well as all the historical evidence we've seen so far, ranging from the impossible technical achievement of the Great Pyramid to historical art depicting our space visitors to an African tribe that has had impossibly precise astronomical knowledge for thousands of years that they say was given to them by beings from a distant star system.

Now you might be shocked by this information but even more surprised and wondering how the government knows of the different species and even what their names are. And here we come to one of the biggest secrets and governmental cover-ups of all. Namely, not only have various extraterrestrial races been visiting Earth for thousands of years, but also the world's major governments at the highest levels have secretly been in physical contact with many of them right here on Earth. And if this one is too difficult for you to believe, there is proof via a multitude of insider whistleblower testimony, a couple of which we turn to now.

The first is an interview that took place on March 5th, 2013 at an undisclosed location within the US, with a terminally ill former CIA officer who had actual physical contact with a "Gray" (one of the species of known extraterrestrials) many years ago during his service.

The officer testifies that he had contact with an extraterrestrial in the flesh and that this was so top secret that even the president of the United States didn't know about it at the time.[37]

Another more intense testimony comes from former US Army Sergeant Clifford Stone, a 22-year veteran who worked for an elite secret group that was dispatched to crash sites to recover extraterrestrial craft and bodies. Sergeant Stone has gone on record testifying that he has personally catalogued 57 species of alien life forms![38]

So as we see, the number given by people like former Defense Minister Paul Hellyer is far short of the full truth because even people in his position were not privy to this ultra-secret information that many times went above the head of the president.

It is well known that Sergeant Stone has never profited financially from releasing such information, and instead has often faced ridicule and attack from the media, which begs the question of why he would testify unless it was the absolute truth and he felt it incredibly important to share it.

Despite the media's and the public's ridicule, there are more and more insiders coming forward each day, and now there are literally hundreds of UFO revelations and direct quotes from people with extremely respectable backgrounds and high positions within the military, the government, NASA, academia, and more. What I've presented here is a very small sample. Could it be that they are *all* lying? That they are *all* crazy? The odds of that are not only infinitesimally small, but also as I've mentioned, when you've worked your whole life to get to such respectable positions, the last thing you would do is risk public humiliation by divulging lies or fantasies. There is so much to be lost and nothing to be gained—unless what you're saying is the truth, and what is to be gained is the truth for all of humanity.

And we have more than just the testimony of these whistleblowers. For instance, when military or commercial pilots claim that they are encountering UFOs moving in ways that defy the laws of known physics and at speeds that are incomprehensible to us, air and ground radar reports often confirm the sightings, according to various documents that have now been officially declassified.

And again, we have numerous highly respected people publicly claiming that this has been ongoing for a very, very long time—in fact, throughout our known history. As Hermann Oberth, an Austro-Hungarian-born German physicist and engineer considered to be one of the founding fathers of rocketry and astronautics, states:

"Flying saucers are real and...they are spaceships from another solar system. I think that they possibly are manned by intelligent observers who are members of a race that may have been investigating our Earth for centuries."[89]

Dr. Brian O'Leary, another former astronaut who is now professor of physics at Princeton University, confirms what everyone else is saying in no uncertain terms after his years of experience and research:

"There is abundant evidence that we are being contacted. That civilizations have been visiting us for a very long time. That their appearance is bizarre from any kind of traditional materialistic western point of view. That these visitors use the technologies of consciousness...that they can manipulate time and space locally so that they can have their own anti-gravity propulsion."[40]

In addition to all the evidence that I've presented here, there are literally *hundreds* of superbly written books on the subject of extraterrestrials and our true place in the cosmos. Once we've shaken off the media conditioning that such topics are of a fringe and non-serious nature, we find that numerous highly respectable people have tackled the subject from various perspectives. From world-famous psychologists at Ivy League universities to renowned archeologists to well-known researchers, there are a host of highly intelligent and respected individuals who have reported on their findings and provided us with undeniable proof from a multitude of scientific fields of investigation.

And so with all of this information, and with evidence spanning thousands of years, up until this very moment, we are left with some very obvious and logical questions. While we may not fully understand all of the hidden government agendas and their goal of keeping all of this a secret, we will naturally find ourselves asking: Who are these advanced extraterrestrial civilizations? What do they have to teach us about the nature of the universe in which we live? Could their technology help alleviate all the environmental and socioeconomic problems we now experience? Could we finally have world peace if we were opened up to a cosmic reality beyond our imaginations that has been hiding right in front of our eyes? And lastly, might they have the answers to many of life's mysteries and some of the remaining hidden keys of existence?

As it turns out, these questions have been answered, and in the next chapter we not only discover the answers, but also combine everything we've learned so far into a cohesive framework, which gives us a readily understandable picture of the true structure of existence.

CHAPTER 6

THE HIDDEN STRUCTURE OF EXISTENCE

"Out beyond ideas of wrongdoing and rightdoing
there is a field. I'll meet you there."

— RUMI

So far we've explored the different aspects of our reality and have begun to see beyond appearances and the filter of belief. We've examined all the scientific evidence that reveals the illusory nature of physical reality and in doing so have started to see it for the grand stage that it really is. We've also peered beyond the veil of physical life to explore the nature of spiritual reality, discovering a world of beautiful energetic realms that we repeatedly visit between each earthly incarnation. And we've uncovered our true cosmic history, realizing that we are not alone as a species in experiencing this wondrous reality.

But now the question is why. Why is physical reality merely a convincing illusion? Why are there vast spirit realms and why do we continually reincarnate into seeming physicality? Why are there countless other species and civilizations and why are they always visiting us?

Although I don't believe that the answers to these questions can be fully understood by our limited human intellect, there is a perspective that can make sense of it all. Of course, this is but one viewpoint, and it cannot be absolute truth, as absolute truth cannot be put into words. Words are symbols that can help point the way to the truth, but the truth can really only ever be experienced directly to be truly understood.

Having said that, symbols can be very helpful, offering us a much-needed structure to help make sense of things. And once we have a deeper understanding, we can readily use that as a portal for accessing the deeper truth that lies just beyond the symbols. Keep this in mind as you read this chapter. What I offer is not a new dogma or belief system, but rather a helpful model of reality based on my years of research and profound personal experiences.

THE INFINITE CREATOR

Assume, if you will, that there exists an infinite Being. There is nothing outside this Being because it is literally infinite. So it is everything and it is One thing simultaneously. It is inherently non-dual. And in non-duality there is no subject and object. There is only Beingness. Assume also that the nature of this infinite, non-dual Being is pure love. But because nothing else exists for this Being to express that love, it is unpotentiated love that is in a state of pure, infinite potential.

So this Being decides that it wants to experience its full potential, and to do that, it splits itself into an infinite number of sub-selves. With that, the universe is born. From undifferentiated formlessness, differentiated form has come forth—and with it duality. Now we have subject and object. We have this *and* that.

But this universe (of seemingly endless differentiation and separation of infinite elements and beings) cannot actually be apart from or outside of its Creator because, by definition, that Creator is infinite. What could exist beyond the limits of infinity when it has no limits by its very definition? And so it's the *illusion* of separation and duality that has been born within this universe. Each seemingly separate element or being now has its own distinct point of view, its own distinct "life" that seems to be apart from its Creator, but in reality, this separation and duality is only illusory. The whole thing is by design because the Creator wants to experience itself from an infinite number of perspectives and experience its true nature (love) in an infinite number of ways.

Although we cannot understand the essence of this infinite Creator intellectually (the concept of infinity is too expansive to be fully grasped by our human minds), as we saw in Chapters 1–3, we do have mounds of scientific proof that every seemingly separate thing is actually one energy vibrating at an infinite number of different frequencies. And as such, we have direct proof of this philosophy that says that the Creator has not simply created everything but actually *is* everything. Indeed, the scientific evidence given us by humanity's greatest geniuses all points to one conclusion: Behind the illusion of duality and separation, there is only One consciousness.

And so what I'm offering here is the idea that we were not simply created by an all-powerful Creator who is completely apart from us and resides in some place separate from us, but rather that we are all literally *aspects* of the One Infinite Creator who encompasses everyone and everything, always. And if you are religious, then I submit to you that God is in everyone and everything because God *is literally everything*; One Consciousness appearing as the entire physical and nonphysical universe and beyond, intertwined and interlinked as One Infinite Essence. And when we allow science to meet spirituality, as we did in Chapters 3–4, we see the proof of this all around us.

THE STRUCTURE OF CREATION

Even if we can understand and accept the idea that we are all the aspects of One Infinite Being and our Creator is not outside us in the sky or in heaven while we are stuck here suffering, we may still wonder how it all works. How is it all structured? Why is there both seemingly physical and nonphysical life? Do we cycle between them endlessly without any ultimate destination? What about all the other life forms in the universe? Do they go through the same journey as us? Are some further ahead on the path and can they teach us something?

As it turns out, there are answers to these questions, and they come from our own ancient spiritual wisdom, as well as that imparted by other more evolved life forms from beyond our planet. What follows is a model of the structure of creation based on the teachings of various independent sources that all essentially say the same thing. Some of these sources are human, some extraterrestrial, and some from beyond the physical altogether. When the source is human, the knowledge is usually derived from profound mystical experiences, near-death experiences, hypnotic regression, and out-of-body experiences. Some of the foremost researchers on this front are Dr. Michael Newton, Dr. Raymond Moody, and Dolores Cannon, as described in Chapter 4.

When the source is extraterrestrial or nonphysical (from an entity that exists purely energetically in the spirit realm), the knowledge is usually transmitted via the process of channeling. During this process, a person enters an altered state of consciousness (sometimes referred to as a meditative trance state) and connects to (or channels) an entity, receiving information telepathically, which is then translated by the human channel through either automatic writing or speaking.

Although there are a number of fakes who claim to be channeling, others have been tested by scientific equipment and their brain waves have been shown to display very different frequencies to that of a normal waking state (scientifically validating the fact that they are not simply making things up and are indeed in a highly altered state of consciousness brought about by a meditative process).[41] In such a non-waking state, the words that they write or speak flow through them automatically without conscious control.

Figure 6.1 depicts a structure of existence that comes together from these various sources, using the terminology of *The Law of One*,[42] which is a highly respected, complex channeled work that perhaps delves most deeply and scientifically into this subject.

Figure 6.1: A density-based model of the hidden structure of existence

Any true model of reality needs to include the science of energy and consciousness to show a firm understanding that the universe is a holographic illusion and not solid as it seems to be; that at the core it is all One consciousness acting as the "body" of the Creator, which only *appears* to be many separate things existing independently of one another. Why is this a must? Because all the evidence confirms it as scientific fact; therefore, a body of work that omits or rejects it cannot serve as a truly unified model of reality. In fact, in this model, physics and metaphysics (science and spirit) are two sides of the same coin.

As you can see from figure 6.1, the universe and creation as a whole consists of multiple planes of existence that vibrate at different energetic frequencies, and each plane is called a "density." According to the channeled teachings, there are seven planes or densities of existence (the exact number varies in different teachings based on the specific definition of densities and the inclusion of sub-densities), with each higher plane being of a higher frequency of energy than the lower planes. But what is the purpose of having different densities?

Remember that the whole physical and nonphysical universe is the "body" that the Creator uses to experience itself from an infinite number of perspectives. The Creator's ultimate reality is pure love and so the whole experience is geared toward growing more and more into the experience of pure, unconditional love. As the Creator creates more and more aspects of its infinite self (you might think of this as the birthing of individual souls), the path of these souls will be to make their way up the densities by learning how to be loving and eventually return to the experience of infinite unconditional love. Each density provides its own unique classroom for soul evolution, with its own set of predominant lessons and states of existence. So the whole meaning of life and the universe itself is to learn the meaning of love in the difficult classrooms that the illusion of duality provides. In doing that we transcend the illusion and return home to our ultimate non-dual nature as the Creator, having expanded in awareness and consciousness, thereby continuing the ever-present impulse for love to expand and give more of itself unto itself.

And with that basic understanding in place, let's delve into the nature and purpose of each density.

THE FIRST DENSITY

The lowest density is the home of all inorganic matter. As we discovered in the first three chapters, everything is conscious. This includes matter that we tend to think of as nonliving, such as the four elements. While this matter may not be alive from a biological definition, it is alive in the sense that it is a form of energy, and therefore of consciousness. Consciousness, in turn, is the body of the Creator within this creation. It is fundamentally aware, down to each atom, as we saw in the double-slit experiment in Chapter 1.

While we may think of ourselves as humans, this is only our current temporary form. Prior to this, we started out by incarnating into the physical realm as the elements. And while this idea may seem strange to us, it makes more sense when we remember that everything is energy and the physical form is but an illusion. Dr. Eben Alexander, the neurosurgeon that we met in Chapter 4, experienced himself during his near-death experience as a single point of consciousness with no self-identity but with an ever-present awareness, nonetheless.[24] That is the experience of first-density existence, which can include hundreds of thousands of different incarnations over a period of millions of years.

THE SECOND DENSITY

The second density is the density of growth, and it is the vibrational plane that plants and animals exist on. Once an individual aspect of consciousness completes its first-density incarnations, it graduates to this second plane of existence, incarnating as plants, trees, and then animals, with each type of incarnation having its own unique experiences and lessons.

Once again, most of us are brought up to view life forms

such as plants to be of lesser value and importance than us. So to think that the consciousness that is incarnate in this human body once experienced itself as a plant might be something we strongly resist or outright reject. But gently put aside any cultural conditioning and remember all we've learned so far. Namely, all physical form is merely illusion. Everything is simply energy. Does energy that organizes into a human have more value than one that organizes into a plant? It's all one and the same thing behind physical appearances. And as we saw in Chapter 3, even the plants are conscious and aware, actively responding to human thoughts. Their main objective in this density, however, is to experience growth and expansion in consciousness as they are now animated with biological life.

THE THIRD DENSITY

The third density is the vibrational plane of consciousness where we currently exist (transitioning to fourth density, but more on that later). Having experienced non-self-aware consciousness and growth, we now incarnate in the human form and experience self-awareness for the first time. And with self-awareness comes choice, which is why this density is often referred to as the density of choice.

By Its very nature of being unconditionally loving, the Creator has created reality in such a way as to give all of Its aspects (i.e., us) free will. Therefore, we aren't forced to express love. Once we've reached this third density, we are presented with a fork in the road and a path to choose. We will either decide to be kind, loving, positive people, or we will decide to be cruel, selfish, negative people. Of course, no one is perfect in this choice, but the question is, which side are you predominantly leaning toward?

If you remember how reincarnation works from Chapter 4, then you know that the tens of thousands of hypnotic regression subjects and NDErs said that there is a life-between-lives plane of existence where we go to consolidate the lessons of each lifetime and then use our free will to plan the next lifetime to include the set of circumstances and events that will most fuel our growth. Our growth toward what? Toward understanding our ultimate true nature as love and returning to it.

And the way we do that is by learning to form a perception that sees everyone and everything as One—that is, to learn unity consciousness. The more we see the unity in everything and realize the illusory nature of separation, the more loving we will naturally be, as we recognize that everything is a part of us and ultimately *is* us.

However, because we have free will, we can choose to focus on our separateness instead of our oneness. This is called separation consciousness. To a large extent, we are all plagued by separation consciousness while in the third density because at this level we feel disconnected from our true Source. Whenever we enter an incarnation in the physical and choose to live another lifetime, there is a veil of forgetfulness that is placed over us so that we take the illusion seriously and have a chance to learn the meaning of true love and compassion in a much more difficult setting in which we think we are actually separate from one another, the planet, and our Creator. Think about how much more meaningful the lesson of love is when you can learn it under such a limited perception. Indeed, it fosters true meaningful growth.

Of course, we can also choose the other extreme of the spectrum and put all of our focus and effort toward building our separation consciousness. Our free will permits this. When that happens, we operate under the principles of fear instead of love because instead of knowing that we are one with, and supported by, the entire universe and our Creator, we feel like we are completely separate and alone. And what's the natural reaction when you feel completely separate and alone? You want to defend yourself. And the best defense is a good offense. So you seek to dominate, manipulate, attack, and control because you think that this will be your fate unless you do it to others first. In *The Law of One* terms, this path is called the service-to-self path. The loving path, by contrast, is called the service-to-others path. More simply, I call them separation consciousness and unity consciousness, respectively.

Now here is the very, very important point to make: The positive path is *not* superior to the negative path. I know that might seem hard to understand, but stay with me. If we understand that we are truly all One, then this naturally includes all the negative, evil, and dark aspects in the universe. Since nothing can exist outside the One Infinite Creator, by definition it is *all* included. Of course, what makes this easier to understand and accept is to realize that evil is ultimately an illusion because it is spawned by nothing but separation consciousness, which is itself illusory, as the reality is that there is no separation. Remember that this is all a grand stage where we get to play out the dance of separation and duality. And remember too that the point of participating on this stage is not to decide who deserves salvation and who deserves condemnation but rather to ultimately reach the only true reality, which is non-dual, infinite love.

Instead of dividing up the world in terms of two camps—the good guys and the bad guys; the righteous and the sinners—it is more helpful to realize that beyond the illusion we are all One. And it's also helpful to realize that the seemingly evil people are serving a much-needed role. For how could we learn the value of love without a seeming evil to practice being loving toward? It's easy to love someone who is very loving. It's a whole other lesson to love someone who is cruel and hurtful. Therefore, those who choose the negative path are, on the one hand, straying from their true natures and forgetting their connections to everything, including the Creator; but on the other hand, they're also indirectly being of service to everyone and the Creator by giving the positive path the chance to learn the true meaning of love in a much deeper and more meaningful fashion.

This brings up the question of punishment. Am I telling you that all evil deeds will go unpunished? Well, not exactly. The various teachings make it clear that the law of karma is very real. Basically, this is a universal law that says that what you put out is what you get back. So if you decide to take the negative path and hurt others, then you will suffer greatly for your choices in a multitude of ways and across subsequent lifetimes. But don't get sucked into what some of the religious leaders would have you believe for their own self-interests. It is not God who judges and punishes evil deeds. God is *everything*, not a separate being watching and judging us. The evil deeds meet their own consequences through the very laws on which a just universe is built. What you put out is what you get back.

Of course, this may make you wonder why bad things happen to good, innocent, loving people. Remember that each of us has lived many lifetimes, and karma does not end when one physical incarnation ends. Therefore, the many seemingly bad things that happen to good people can simply be karmic rebalancing, and the ones who they are happening to are *not* victims. Always keep in mind the idea of free will and the fact that each of us *chooses* our life and all the major events that will unfold in it before we incarnate. We know the hurt we have caused others in previous lives and therefore we often choose difficult circumstances to give ourselves the opportunity to experience what others experienced, and thereby grow in compassion from the greater perspective afforded by these experiences.

So to conclude our exploration of the most difficult density, we are ultimately choosing either the path of developing unity consciousness and the desire to love and serve one another, or separation consciousness and the desire to selfishly hurt and dominate others. Most of us tend to choose the former, positive path, while a minority chooses the latter path, simultaneously acting as our oppressors and (unconsciously) as our greatest teachers on how to love unconditionally.

As we turn our attention to the higher densities, it's important to understand that they are invisible to us since they exist on a higher vibrational level that we can't perceive. Some people have the ability to perceive the higher densities with one or more of their senses, and at times beings from these densities can choose to phase down their energetic frequency to make themselves perceptible, but in general these higher planes of existence are all but invisible to the limited programming of the receiver/transmitter that we call the human brain.

THE FOURTH DENSITY

While the third density is the density of choice, the fourth density is known as the density of love. On this plane of existence, those who have "graduated" or "ascended" get to experience the fruits of their labor. If we have chosen the positive path and learned to be loving, then when our reincarnation lessons in the third density are over, we move on to either fourth-density Earth (as the entire planet's consciousness shifts, which I'll share in the next chapter) or another fourth-density planet.

From our contact with various positive fourth-density civilizations (through channelings or rare direct contact with a small number of people), we know that fourth-density reality on the positive path is quite different than ours. It is what we might think of as a utopia or paradise. The limiting emotions of anger, jealousy, lust, greed, sadness, and so on, are released as they have been transcended and are no longer needed for learning purposes. Now, the focus is on developing the ability to truly love. Fourth-density civilizations are therefore telepathic societies, where everyone is connected as a harmonious collective in unity consciousness; and yet, within that, individuality is honored and nurtured. This makes sense, as unconditional love is inclusive and fully accepting. And because the entire society is connected telepathically, it is impossible to be dishonest or deceitful. As such, there is no crime, no violence, and no war. It is truly a utopian state of existence where we get to experience numerous incarnations (whether as humans or other evolved humanoid life forms) dedicated to growing our understanding and application of unconditional love.

For those on the negative path, they also eventually graduate, but theirs is far from joyous. These souls move on to fourth-density planets that have a strong collective separation consciousness. These are highly oppressive environments where violence and war rage on. We could think of them as hellish worlds. The human souls that move on to incarnate on such worlds are not being "punished" by God for their deeds on Earth, but simply experiencing the universal law of karma. They are reaping what they sowed, and it is their chosen path by their own free will. There also seem to be hellish realms beyond the physical realms, and we know this not only from channeled material but also from near-death experience research, most notably the work of highly respected researcher Nancy Evans Bush who, after 30 years of exhaustive research, wrote the landmark book *Dancing Past the Dark: Distressing Near-Death Experiences.*[43]

In essence, the research tells us that many people have received glimpses of hellish realms through near-death experiences. And for the instant skeptics (I was previously one regarding this subject), it is interesting to note that Dr. Alexander, who I mentioned in Chapter 4 and who had no brain wave activity whatsoever that could even cause any imagination or hallucination to possibly take place, also visited a "hellish" realm during his journey that later took his consciousness to a heavenly realm, scientifically confirming (for the first time ever) the validity of the potential existence of "hell."[24]

However, it is very important to understand that this is not the religious concept of hell that says that God punishes sinners for eternity. Once again, understood in the correct scientific/spiritual context, it is a *temporary* realm of karmic rebalancing, where those who have inflicted great pain on others experience the consequences of their free will actions. So this is not "judgment" that says these bad souls don't deserve the love of the Creator. It is simply a universal mechanism of learning, which is still *within* the Creator, and the souls experiencing the learning are still aspects who are an integral part of their Creator—that is, even this is a part of the experience that Infinite Intelligence

113

chooses to go through, and it is just as valid as any other experience—although not as comfortable or enjoyable. And in case you're worried, *The Law of One* teachings make it clear that only people who are extremely negative (95 percent of the way on the extreme negative side of the spectrum) will need to experience such realms for their karmic rebalancing (which will be very unbalanced given how much pain they caused others).

Getting back to the fourth density, the interesting thing here is that the fourth density is still considered the density of love, even for the negative path, but it is not an unconditionally selfless love on that path. Rather, it is a purely selfish love; the love of self above all else. This is not the ultimate true love but fear masquerading as love. Those who love themselves selfishly and exclusively are doing so out of an incredible amount of fear. They are in the depths of fear because they feel completely separate and cut off from everything, including their Source. The reality is that no one can actually be cut off from the Source, but they can *believe* that they are and therefore experience this to be their truth. The vast majority of souls, however, choose the positive path while in third density, and therefore their experience in fourth density is one of beautiful, selfless love.

THE FIFTH DENSITY

Once the fourth-density lessons are sufficiently learned through numerous incarnations, beings and even entire planets graduate to the fifth density, which is the density of wisdom. Now the lesson is to grow in universal knowledge and understanding. The positive fifth-density civilizations use this knowledge to help and be in service to other worlds, while the negative ones use it to dominate other worlds (usually third-density planets that still need to learn the lessons of love). In the fifth-density plane, bodies become quasi-physical in preparation for the sixth density.

THE SIXTH DENSITY

At this density, beings predominantly incarnate as non-physical entities (although they can choose to take physical form if and when they choose). At that point, they have released all sense of a separate self, and merge into a wondrous and blissful collective self. Essentially, they become an entire planetary consciousness that merges together as one identity. At that point they no longer experience themselves as individual souls like we currently do, but instead merge into a collective that experiences much more of the true unity behind all beings.

The interesting thing here is that the negative path reunites with the positive at the sixth density. How does that happen? How do seemingly evil beings suddenly become positive? Remember that the fifth density is the density of wisdom, and by the end of it, those beings have learned enough universal wisdom that the ultimate truth finally dawns on them. They realize that they can evolve no further if they stay on the negative path, and their strong desire for evolution causes them to undergo an instantaneous and complete transformation for the positive.

Again, we've become so accustomed to thinking about sin and evil that it can be hard to understand how such beings could be "rewarded" with the heavenly existence of blissful consciousness. But keep in mind the reality of Infinite Oneness that lies behind the entire illusion of separation. This reality is not theory and is not something we are simply told by the channeled teachings. Think back to Chapter 1 and to how even our science is conclusively proving that separation is an illusion. And also remember that the whole point of this exercise called existence is *not* to separate the good from the bad and to see who deserves God's love and approval and who deserves condemnation. Rather, it is to experience every possible perspective and to gain every possible experience on the way to expanding and reuniting with the infinite non-dual love that we all truly are. Given this, it is understood that *everyone* eventually ends up in the same place. *All beings* eventually end up reuniting with the Creator, and no one is left out because the Creator is by definition all-inclusive and not separate from the creation. The only thing that differs between beings is the path they take to get home. Some take an easier positive path, and some take an excruciatingly difficult negative path, but the latter group has suffered so much by the time they reach the sixth density that they have rebalanced all the karma they had accumulated from hurting others for so long.

Really think about all of this and you realize that it makes so much more sense to view the Creator in this way rather than to think of "him" as a separate judgmental being. The word *unconditional* cannot in any way be stated in the same sentence as judgment. You cannot say that God loves unconditionally while also saying that God judges and punishes. The statement is an oxymoron. The two qualities cannot simultaneously exist, for judgment and punishment imply conditions. This is not to say that there is no justice in the Creator's universe. There is justice, but that justice comes in the form of karmic law that simply rebalances energy and acts as a teacher of love to each seemingly separate soul rather than there being a judgmental Creator who is vengeful and angry at those who don't follow his will that is seemingly separate from theirs. And how much more profound is this definition of an infinite, unconditionally loving Creator that encompasses all than the definition of a separate, finite, conditionally judgmental Creator?

THE SEVENTH DENSITY

We know very little about the seventh density, as beings that have made it to this plane of existence have reached such a state of near completion and timelessness that they are getting ready to reunite with the One Infinite Creator and fully realize their identity as All That Is. They are now pure consciousness, or possibly even non-dual awareness beyond all consciousness (which implies the existence of subject and object). And in essence, this is the journey we all take. It is a journey without distance, returning home to our true Self, forever One beyond time and space.

DIRECT EVIDENCE FROM NASA

If you haven't previously come across any of this information and this is all seeming a bit "out there," I understand. We've been told all our lives that we are alone on this planet and in the universe (certainly in our solar system), and it may be very difficult to accept the reality that advanced and much more evolved civilizations not only exist but are also communicating with us and even sharing the secrets of the universe and existence with us. But evidence, direct from NASA, seems to confirm some of the information that is contained in many of the channeled material from extraterrestrial and extra-dimensional sources.

As an example, let's look at the evidence that supports the claims made by *The Law of One* channeled material, which again is the most thoroughly scientific in its description of the structure of the universe. The source of *The Law of One* claims to be a sixth-density collective consciousness that used to exist as a physical society as it made its way up through the third, fourth, and fifth densities. They say they originated more than two billion years ago and left artifacts (such as pyramids, obelisks, and other monuments) all over our solar system, many of which they say still stand to this day.

Those are some incredible claims, and we might be prone to dismissing them due to their seemingly sensational nature. Luckily, a few brilliant investigative researchers have probed deeper into the photos released by NASA over the years and noticed some very interesting anomalies. Of course, we rarely hear about these findings because it doesn't take a huge leap of imagination to realize that certain corporations and governments have a vested interest in keeping the existence of extraterrestrials (and their highly advanced technologies) a secret. Nevertheless, enough respected researchers have written books and done entire presentations on them that we actually have a body of evidence showing that these ancient relics actually exist and that highly advanced, ancient extraterrestrial civilizations had previously colonized our entire solar system, just like various channeled material such as *The Law of One* claim. The following is a small sample of images reproduced from David Wilcock's monumental book *The Ascension Mysteries*,[44] which delves much deeper into this subject.

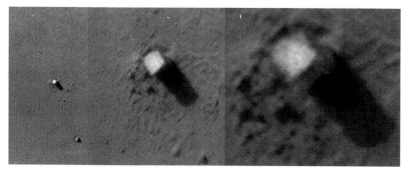

Figure 6.2 The monolith on Phobos
(lunar surface of one of the moons of Mars)

As you can see from the NASA photograph in Figure 6.2, there is a very clear unnatural object built on the face of this moon (one of the moons of Mars), which is rectangular (nature does not produce rectangles) and metallic, and casting a long shadow. This is an extremely clear picture that provides very convincing evidence of an unnatural monument, which seems to confirm the public statement given by NASA astronaut Buzz Aldrin of an existence of a monolith structure on one of the moons of Mars.[44]

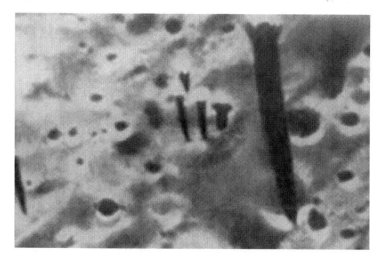

Figure 6.3 Original NASA Lunar Orbiter 2 Image
LO2–61H3 showing lunar obelisks

Figure 6.3 presents a photograph of our own moon (the backside of the moon that we never get to see), and it very clearly shows the shadows of six large obelisk structures (resembling the Washington, DC, monument). Nature does not produce obelisk structures like this, and it has left many mainstream scientists baffled. Archeologists have noted that it looks precisely like prehistoric archeological sites, and other scientists have even wanted to call this region on the moon "the Valley of Monuments," according to Wilcock.[44] This shows how clear it is that this is not a natural phenomenon we are observing.

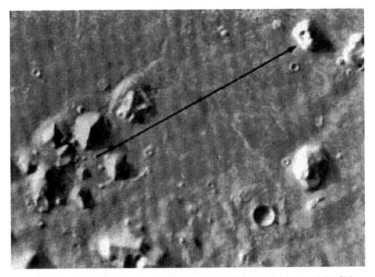

Figure 6.4 Close-up of NASA Viking Frame 35A76
showing the face and pyramids on Mars

Finally, in this stunning NASA photograph shown in Figure 6.4, we can clearly see a massive monument of a face on the surface of Mars at the top right. Looking left, we see an entire "city" of pyramids. Nature also doesn't create perfect pyramids. What's even more interesting, as David Wilcock notes, is that researcher

Richard C. Hoagland has used scientific evidence to show that the face is an artificially constructed, mile-wide monument with symmetrical human features and that the pyramid cluster has the proportions of Leonardo da Vinci's *Vitruvian Man*.[44] Indeed, photographic experts, independent scientists, and mathematicians have studied these pictures and found some incredible symmetries that they indicate are clearly artificial in nature.

A MAGICAL WORLD

So as you see, just as *The Law of One* and other respected channeled material claim, there are indeed artifacts all over our solar system. This not only proves that we are not alone but also, when combined with the massive amount of corroborating evidence and other scientific proof, builds the legitimacy and credibility of the channeled material and the information it teaches us about our world and the structure of reality.

What we discover when we are open to questioning our previously held beliefs is that nothing is as we were told. Far from being a boring existence, we live in a magical world without knowing it. All around us are intelligent civilizations, other realms, various dimensions, and a precisely designed structure to guide it all forward in an evolutionary impulse that is leading us all back to the heart of creation, which is the home we never left in reality. This is not the stuff of science-fiction movies and fantasy film. This is real life.

And with that in mind, let's take all we've learned so far and get practical. How can all of this knowledge truly transform our lives? Can this hidden reality be tapped into in our practical everyday life, leading us to the joy, peace, and true fulfillment we've always searched for? And if so, is there any hope for change in the world at large?

In Part II, we'll delve into these subjects, beginning with the cosmic shift that has already begun, and then get into the personal specifics of how to live an awakened life and experience love and peace like you've never known it before.

PART II

AWAKENING

"Your vision will become clear only when you can look into your own heart. Who looks outside, dreams; who looks inside, awakes."

— CARL JUNG

CHAPTER 7

THE SHIFT

"The Golden Age is before,
not behind us."

– WILLIAM SHAKESPEARE

There is some good news for us all. This crazy world that we live in is about to exit the insane asylum. Some level of insanity often characterizes third-density planets because we are still learning how to be loving on this plane of existence, while seemingly disconnected from our Source. The illusion of separation is very strong at this level, which creates fear and leads to conflict. As such, what we get is a very challenging learning environment for the souls that incarnate here. But that's all about to change.

You may have heard about the Mayan calendar that ended in December 2012. Many people prophesized the end of the world at that time, which obviously did not come to pass. But is there something more to this mysterious calendar that is revered by so many (including a large number of respected scientists)? The short answer is a loud and resounding *yes*.

QUANTUM LEAPS IN EVOLUTION

As it turns out, some modern astronomers have discovered the existence of a 25,920-year orbit that our entire solar system makes around a neighboring brown dwarf star (a star that is very difficult to see even with advanced telescopes).[45] By measuring the effects of gravitational pull, they have discovered that our sun likely exists as part of a binary star system (i.e., two suns orbiting each other).

The Mayans were already well aware of this phenomenon, and their entire calendar was built on it. This 25,920-year cycle, which the Mayans called the "Great Year," was further broken down into 12 equal cycles of 2,160 years each, which have come to be known as the "Ages of the Zodiac." What the Mayan calendar shows is that December 2012 was the end of one of these ages, the Age of Pisces, and the beginning of the next, the Age of Aquarius. More importantly, it also marked the end of an entire 25,920-year cycle.

By now it seems clear that all of these ancient cultures had more advanced knowledge of the cosmos than we do today with all of our technology, and seems to point very clearly to some sort of interaction with highly advanced extraterrestrial civilizations that shared knowledge with them. And perhaps more relevant to us is that if we study world history, we see that some truly incredible changes occur at the end of these grand cycles.

David Wilcock, the brilliant researcher of consciousness and ancient civilizations discusses this phenomenon in his book *The Synchronicity Key: The Hidden Intelligence Guiding the Universe and You*, and describes the solid scientific evidence that human evolution is moving according to this 25,920-year cycle.[45] Namely, if we look back around 50,000 years in history (i.e., two cycles back), then we find that something very strange occurred. Prior to that, no one on Earth used any tool more sophisticated than a crude stone blade. But anthropologists have discovered that right at this time, people around the world suddenly started making musical instruments, artwork, religious carvings, harpoons, arrowheads, needles, and beaded jewelry.

Imagine that. Suddenly evolving from using crude tools to sophisticated and artistic developments, at the same time, all around the world. How could this possibly happen? These ancient societies—separated by huge landmasses and entire oceans—had no contact with one another. And yet, despite that, they all suddenly started making music, art, jewelry, and weapons in very similar ways at the same time? Quite clearly, this was not the product of the painfully slow random evolution theory we've been taught to believe in. Everyone around the world just seemed to get a massive IQ boost at the same time, suddenly becoming much more intelligent. The odds against this being random evolution is billions to one.

So what happened at the last cycle, around 26,000 years ago? That was precisely when the Neanderthals disappeared. Most anthropologists are absolutely baffled by their extinction, and have been unable to find the missing link between the Neanderthals and humans. But what if the Neanderthals didn't just die out but were rather *transformed* into modern-day humans? Once again, by conventional evolution theory, this could not have taken place within such a short span of time. It would take millions of years before that kind of giant evolutionary shift could occur. And yet it happened quite suddenly.

So what's going on here? It seems that instead of the slow, random evolution espoused by Charles Darwin, where adaptation and mutation occurs over very long periods of time, what has actually happened is instantaneous *quantum leaps* in evolution over only one or two generations. And even more interestingly, they have been happening at about 26,000-year intervals.

How could this be? This isn't what we were taught in school. But by now you shouldn't be too surprised that reality is quite different than what we've been taught. Indeed, most respected non-mainstream (i.e., non-corporate-controlled) scientists, tell us that Darwin's theory of evolution has literally countless holes in it,[46] and any one of them could completely dismantle the entire theory.

This isn't to say that there is no evolution or that everything doesn't evolve. Not at all. Simply that evolution is not necessarily a gradual random process of adaptation and survival of the fittest. As it turns out, it's not random at all, and it certainly isn't systematically gradual. The theory is disproven not only by sudden quantum leaps in evolution but also in the many species without a prior evolutionary link and, more obviously, in the fact that we have absolutely no fossil records of the "inferior" part of the species.[46] These are the species that didn't fit the "survival of the fittest" test and therefore didn't evolve into the new species that we presently see. We should be discovering their fossils but they are nowhere to be found.

The Sun's Hidden Power

And so, the logical question we're left with is this: If evolution has evidently been making sudden quantum leaps in precise grand cycles, and we've just completed such a cycle in 2012, then what is going to happen now? And what exactly will cause it to happen?

The answers to that are marvelously laid out in various books by highly respected researchers, most notably David Wilcock's *The Synchronicity Key*.[45] In it, he amasses a giant body of research from independent scientists around the world showing that our entire evolution is intimately tied to our sun. Indeed, scientists such as Alexander Tchijevsky have very conclusively demonstrated that sunspot activity has a direct, powerful effect on humankind. He studied a 2,500-year period of world history and found, to his astonishment, that 80 percent of the most significant events in our history occurred during peak periods of sunspot activity that exhibited massive solar flares.

When this is coupled with the research from Wilcock's prior landmark book *The Source Field Investigations*, which showed how light photons directly affect DNA, we arrive at a very significant and surprising conclusion: The sun causes the quantum shifts in evolution we see at the end of the 26,000 year cycles. More specifically, various scientific studies have conclusively proven that light has the ability to change DNA structure at a fundamental level. The most incredible of such studies, as Wilcock noted, came from DNA specialist Dr. Peter Gariaev.[7]

Dr. Gariaev performed experiments in which he changed one species into another by manipulating the DNA with light. Basically, he sent a green laser through salamander eggs and then redirected the beam into frog eggs, with the astonishing result that the frog eggs transformed into salamander eggs. And he later found that although these salamanders were created from the genes of frogs, they lived normally as salamanders and could breed with other salamanders to produce normal, healthy offspring. He later tried this experiment with various other eggs and was able to replicate it successfully, literally transforming one species into another using the light from a special laser.

Now you would think that this kind of discovery would make world headline news. But most of us heard nothing of it. When an independent scientist discovers something that threatens to shake up humanity's worldview and lead to some important conclusions that would positively transform the world, the powers that be seem to stifle it with their control of mainstream science and media.

But all of that is about to change. When you tie these discoveries together, you come to an absolutely incredible conclusion: namely, if it has been conclusively proven that light can change the very structure of DNA, and it has also been proven that the source of light (our sun) has a direct influence on the rise and fall of civilizations around the world, then could it not be that the sun is what's responsible for the quantum shifts in evolution that we see occurring approximately every 26,000 years?

It is rather probable that at the completion (within a timeframe of a number of years) of each of these grand cycles, the sun gives off solar flares of gigantic proportions that have the power to change the DNA structure of *every* living thing on this planet, including us. Such an event would very adequately explain how humans suddenly got a huge intelligence boost 50,000 years ago and how Neanderthal man suddenly disappeared and possibly transformed into modern man around 25,000 years ago.

WHAT HAPPENS NOW?

But if we just completed another 25,920-year cycle, then shouldn't something be happening now? As it turns out, scientists have been noticing much higher amounts of energy being emitted by the sun in recent years, and certain physicists—most notably the German physicist Deiter Broers, who is behind the documentary

Solar Revolution—believe that a world-changing event of some sort is imminent.[47]

So what kind of quantum leap in evolution could be in store for us this time around? Many prominent scientists believe it will be nothing less than a gradual build up of incredible abilities, such as telepathy (communication via thought), telekinesis (the ability to move objects with our mind), levitation, and more. But much more important than these fringe benefits is what it means in spiritual terms. According to sources such as *The Law of One*, the way planets shift into the higher densities is through a mechanism controlled by each planet's sun, which emits huge amounts of high vibrational energy through giant solar flares at the end of each cycle. This means that the giant sun flares will not only change physical life as we know it, but will also mark a shift into fourth-density Earth on the spiritual front.

Of course, this is great cause for celebration. If you remember, the fourth density is the density of love, wherein planets exist in a state of utopia, as the beings shift to the lesson of learning pure, unconditional love in this higher vibrational state of existence. As Earth shifts to a fourth-density planet, therefore, it will be shifting to the Golden Age of humanity that has been prophesied by so many spiritual and religious traditions throughout history. In fact, as David Wilcock has discovered after exhaustive research spanning 20 years, 35 different religions and spiritualties have prophecies within them about this coming Golden Age.

Of course for the minority who are on the negative, service-to-self path, this event will not be welcomed. That's because the massive solar flares will contain huge amounts of high vibrational "positive" energy that is needed to shift the planet to the positive fourth density, and anyone with very negative energy will be unable to cope with it. It may very likely cause psychological breakdowns and other issues. This could be why some religious traditions have called it the "Day of Judgment."

Once again, I note my belief that religious leaders may have misrepresented this idea in order to create fear and obedience. In my opinion, it is not the day that God's wrath will befall us (for how could an unconditionally loving Creator express the highly limited human emotion of wrath), but rather a natural evolutionary demarcation point that will act as a literal fork in the road, which will simply separate the negative and positive paths. Remember this is the density of choice, and at the end of it we deal with the consequences of that choice.

Of course, the good news for those with a positive orientation is that the shift will be a positive, transformative experience, in which we will go through a process of gradually shedding much of our limiting emotions and have a spiritual quantum leap of sorts.

It's not clear from the channeled teachings, the science, or the religious prophecies exactly *how* this event will take place and over what time period. What *does* seem to be quite clear, however, is that we will all know when the solar flares have occurred because everyone on Earth will feel that something very significant and unprecedented has happened, and it will be the trigger that will start the massive gradual shift into the prophesized Golden Age. The actual world changes may take many years to fully play out, as this will be more of a process than a one-time event, but they may well include worldwide disclosure of extraterrestrial presence, a release of the free energy and healing technologies that have been suppressed by corporations for so long, a complete restructuring of the financial system to make it much more equitable, release of advanced antigravity vehicles (currently known as UFOs), and with all of that, an effective end to world hunger, disease, war, and environmental destruction.

WE HAVE A PART TO PLAY

But there's one crucial thing to understand. This Golden Age won't just happen by itself, but rather needs to be *triggered* by our collective consciousness.

As you'll recall, behind the illusion of separation everything in the universe is actually connected. So this physical/spiritual quantum evolutionary leap is intimately connected to our collective consciousness. If our mass consciousness had evolved positively enough, then the shift to this ideal reality would have been triggered at the end of the last cycle in 2012. But there's a window of time between the end of one cycle and the beginning of the next. We are in that crucial moment in history right now.

As I mentioned, every major religion and spiritual teaching prophesied the coming of this Golden Age, and these spiritual teachings are often either given directly from extra-dimensional sources or influenced by them. And since these sources are from beyond our space-time continuum and therefore can clearly see our future time lines, it likely means that we can be assured that the shift will occur, and a Golden Age will be heralded within the coming few years.

But this doesn't mean we can just sit around and wait to be saved. The Golden Age has occurred in our future timeline precisely *because* of the awakening that is happening now. And each of us has the responsibility—and honor—to play a part in this beautiful shift and make it happen. When we become disheartened when we watch the news and see all the negative things happening around the world, we can remember that this is not an accurate reflection of the state of the world. Earth is a much more positive environment than we think it is—we simply get only the negative stuff shoved in our faces night and day. And while most of the world's problems are due to a tiny minority of elites who have a lot less power than they would like us to believe, it is we who give them their power, and it is we who can just as easily take it back.

It is also wise to remember that the majority of us are positive, and positive energy is integrative, naturally building on itself, while negative energy naturally disintegrates—as you discovered in wave coherence in Chapter 1 (see figure 1.4). This means that one truly positive person is enough to outweigh up to 1,000 or more negative individuals. This is not merely wishful thinking but has been shown in experiments with meditators (see the study of the 7,000 meditators who affected the entire world, in Chapter 2); and also proven by luminaries such as Gandhi, who was able to defeat an entire army due to his incredibly high level of consciousness, which harnessed the positive energy of the masses and brought an empire to its knees.

So as you see, the Golden Age really is all in our hands. Only a lack of knowledge and negative conditioning has brought about any disempowerment we may currently feel. But conditioning can be changed and with it the world transformed. And to help you be a direct part of this change, I would like to humbly offer you my guidance. I have been a student and practitioner of spirituality for 15 years, and although I am by no means perfect and still make many mistakes, I am dedicated to living a life based on kindness and love and therefore have much practice with it. It is my sincere hope that the following chapters, as well as the Awakening Practices at the end of each one (including this chapter), can be of great use to you in transforming your life and our world.

AWAKENING PRACTICES

The following practices can be done any time. I recommend you spend at least 5–10 minutes on each one, staying with it for as long as you'd like. If you resonate deeply with one or both, you might choose to make it a daily practice. Each awakening practice was created to help you apply the knowledge you're learning, and so raise your consciousness and deepen your connection to the truth of your being.

Before starting each practice, silence your phone and try to make sure that you won't be disturbed. Sit or lie down in a comfortable position, close your eyes, and gently begin.

THE EMBRACE OF LOVE

The purpose of this practice is to develop your experience of unconditional love for everyone in the world. Expressing unconditional love in our everyday lives is not always easy, especially when we're tested by those that we don't like or perceive to be the enemies of our peace, so this practice is meant to help you gradually build this skill in a safe, internal environment.

- Take several deep breaths, relaxing with each one, and then let your breathing return to its normal rhythm.

- Feel your body, experiencing the physical and emotional sensations, and allow them to simply be there. Gently, place your focus on your heart and let a feeling of warm love grow there. If it helps you to think of someone you truly love, you may wish to start with that, but let the love expand to a more abstract love that simply loves by its very nature, without needing an object to express that love towards. From this place of unconditional love, expand outward and let that love embrace your entire body.

- Then gently let it embrace all your surroundings. Let it expand to embrace your entire home and anyone in it, seeing them being embraced by this love. Then to your neighborhood and those in it. Then to your entire city, covering it and all its residents with a blanket of love.

- Expand this love outward to your whole country. Be sure to think of people you dislike or even hate (both those you know and public figures), and let that love embrace them too. If you have difficulty in doing this, remember that behind the illusion they, like you, are love itself, and they've merely forgotten their true nature and strayed from their Source.

- Continue letting that love spread across the globe, to all nations and people, and to nature and the animals too. Let it embrace everyone and everything equally.

- And now that your limitless love has covered the Earth, let all that love turn around and embrace you in loving gratitude. Let the love that everyone truly is beyond the veil of separation envelop your very being.

- Rest in that love for as long as you desire.

A New World

In this practice, you'll be visualizing the ideal world we all wish existed. When enough people desire and truly see this future as a real possibility, it will trigger the energetic shift on our planet, and with it the quantum leap in evolution we discussed in this chapter. When you use this practice, you are not merely fantasizing, but rather using the laws of consciousness to alter reality and help bring about the world you want to live in.

- Take several deep breaths, relaxing with each one, and then let your breathing return to its normal rhythm.

- In your mind's eye, begin to visualize a world that is worthy of being called the Golden Age. This world is the reality you want to co-create with your fellow human beings who are of a unity consciousness. A world without poverty. A world without hunger. A world without war, violence, or injustice. Visualize a world where disease and sickness do not exist, and we honor the earth and the animals.

- Immerse yourself in this world of harmony, love, and peace—a true Golden Age where humanity is one. See how there is no need for countries or borders, and feel what it would be like if there were a pervading spirit of unity and a deep connection among all people, as each understands that self and others are One in truth.

- Look around this world and see how there is no need for money, as this is a world of abundance where highly advanced technology is used in harmony with nature, giving us free clean energy, food, water, and shelter. It is a world in which everyone follows their passion and creates, sharing freely with everyone else. All prosper and grow perpetually from this love and selfless giving.

- This is the coming new world and as you visualize it in intricate detail and infuse those images with strong joyful emotion, you are using the energy of thought to help make it happen.

- Stay with this visualization as long as you desire.

CHAPTER 8
THE AWAKENED LIFE

"Ego says, 'Once everything falls into place,
I'll feel peace.' Spirit says, 'Find your peace,
and then everything will fall into place.'"

– MARIANNE WILLIAMSON

It's a very common and natural reaction for those who wake up to the true nature of reality and the choice at hand in the third density to want to get busy being more positive. We want to help others, fight injustice, and change the world for the better. We want to hurry along the shift to the Golden Age and be free of war, poverty, and environmental destruction so that we can all live in peace and harmony. On a more personal level, we may also want to change our career or certain relationships that are keeping us stuck. But while all these things are wonderful, we need to avoid falling into the trap of putting doing before *being*.

What do I mean by that? Remember the *purpose* of this whole illusion we call reality in the first place. There is one and only one goal we all ultimately have: to learn to become unconditionally loving and return home to our true essence, having expanded the spark of divinity that we all are. And when looked at from this higher perspective, we realize that *what* we do in the illusion is always secondary to *how* and *why* we do it. A parent who is unconditionally loving with their children and truly gentle and kind to others on a daily basis is doing more to help free the world of tyranny than someone who is heading a massive nonprofit organization that fights injustice on a global scale, but is doing so with anger and hatred in their heart.

Now that may seem to be a controversial statement and it cannot be understood by aligning with the world's usual way of thinking. But when looked at from the perspective of the true nature of reality and the very purpose of existence, it makes all the sense in the world. More precisely, the person who is fighting injustice in the world on a grand scale but doing so with anger and hatred in their heart is not only *not learning* the only lesson they're here to learn, but also contributing to the problem by adding more negative energy to the planet. Sure, they may be alleviating the suffering of others, and that is helpful, but they're doing it in a way that ensures the destructive cycle of hate, and therefore the very problem they're fighting against, stays alive. If we try to fight injustice with hate, we only add fuel to the fire and can never bring about the lasting meaningful change we desire.

BEING OF SERVICE TO THE WORLD

Given all of this, the conclusion becomes very clear: To transform our lives and the world, we need to come from a place of love and compassion, even as we act to "fight" injustice. We need to let our *being inspire our doing*. When our hearts are filled with love and a genuine desire to be of service to others, then whatever needs to be done will naturally arise in the most helpful way possible. More than that, it will be exponentially more helpful than if we angrily wage internal and external war on injustice, seeing the perpetrators in the same light that they see the people they oppress.

Each of us has chosen to come into this life with a certain set of talents that can be used to be of service to others. It could be something as simple as being a patient and nonjudgmental listener. It could be that you are artistic and your art touches people on a deep level. It could be that you are a great leader who can effect real, meaningful change. Or, you may have a gift of writing or making music or cooking or healing. The list is endless. But no natural talent or skill is fundamentally more important than another, even if one skill seems to touch thousands of people and another only a few, because the reality is that separation is only an illusion anyway, and there's really only One of us here appearing to be many. Keeping this very real science and spirituality in mind will help to keep you from falling into the trap of feeling like you need to do something big and far-reaching to be of true service.

The other equally important thing to understand is that our greatest service and primary purpose in life is to be our true Self. That's it.

We are conditioned to believe that living a truly meaningful life means we need to make something of ourselves or leave a legacy. But these are egocentric thoughts that stem from an unconscious feeling of unworthiness. The only reason we seek worldly success and recognition, or a desire to leave a name for ourselves, is because we don't feel we're enough as we already are. Even the seemingly humble desire to leave a good name for being a good and honest person stems, in the ultimate sense, from a deep-seated sense of unworthiness. Think about it. Why would we care about being recognized by others unless we didn't feel complete as we already are? And do you see that separating the world into those who are good and honest (our camp) and those who aren't (their camp) does nothing but invite a feeling of superiority because we're in the good camp and they're not? This, in fact, is often the essence behind religious fundamentalism, which professes forgiveness but really does nothing but judge and condemn.

The traps of the physical self that we think we are (often referred to as the "ego-self") are as subtle as they are many. The ultimate reality is that we are *already* whole and complete. Maybe not on this level, but this person who we think we are is not really us. We are not humans who have temporary spiritual experiences. We are Spirit having a temporary human experience. And although on the ultimate level, beyond the seventh plane of existence, we are truly perfect and One, on the third density, we are still learning how to express our true perfect essence. And because time is but an illusion and postulated to be so by various highly respected scientists such as Albert Einstein, everything ultimately exists *simultaneously*. We only appear to be moving forward in time, evolving as an individual soul, learning lessons of love, and slowly perfecting ourselves.

In reality, we exist in all states in the eternal now, which is all there really is. And because of that, there's really nothing to strive for or to feel inadequate about. You are worthy of unconditional love just as you are *now*. Even with all of your seeming imperfections and all the unloving acts you do, you are worthy. That's the meaning of the word *unconditional*. There's nothing you have to prove to deserve love. You're already there, at the finish line, behind the illusion. Your only role is to be a conduit of experience to the Infinite Self that you truly are, which wishes nothing but to experience itself from an infinite number of perspectives and to expand from this experience.

And how do you do that? By simply being the expression of the love that you already are as best you can. That is our real mission. And every other mission you may have is secondary to simply learning how to express your Beingness as purely as possible, reflecting the unconditional love that is your ultimate nature. When you do that you are being of utmost service to the world and living the awakened life, because you are putting *being* first and letting doing be inspired from that calm center of the true Self.

THE SUBTLE TRAPS

While we can have the intention to put being our true Self first, there are some subtle traps along this path, and if we're not careful it's very easy to fall into them. So let's bring them to the light of awareness so we may safely navigate through them.

TRAP #1: HAPPINESS VERSUS TRUE FULFILLMENT

If you ask people what they want most in life, the usual answer is "to be happy." Sure, there can be many other things we want, like romantic love, a close family, children, success, money, material possessions, and so on, but behind each of these things is the simple desire to be happy. We want these things because we believe they will make us happy. And while of course there's nothing wrong with any of these things in and of themselves, believing that they bring true happiness can be a major trap that keeps us unfulfilled on the deepest levels and holds us back from living out our true life purpose.

To understand why this is so, we have to make the distinction between happiness and true fulfillment. This thing called happiness, that we chase so compulsively our entire lives, is often nothing more than the internal demand that screams, "Meet my desires!" We all have objects of desire, and while some of them can seem very noble—like deep romantic love or a close family and children—equating them with happiness will ultimately lead us away from true fulfillment at the soul level. The reason for this is that we are grasping for something outside ourselves to "give us" that happiness we seek. When we want something badly, we are basically saying, "I'll only be happy *if* I get what I want." In the case of romantic love, we're saying, "I'll only be truly happy *if* I find someone who I love and who loves me as much." In the case of a family and children, we're saying, "I'll only be happy *if* I have a close family and children who I love and who love me back."

Of course, these things seem natural to us. We may understand what's wrong with desiring money and material possessions so strongly that we associate happiness with their attainment, but we don't tend to look at it the same way with the things that most societies and cultures value so strongly, such as true love and family. But the problem with all of this is not the things we desire (true love and family can be beautiful things); it's the fact that we give them complete power over us by equating their attainment with happiness. And what happens when you give something the power to provide you happiness? It can just as easily take away that happiness and bring pain and suffering.

Think about it, how many "true-love" relationships end in heartbreak? And even if they are the "real thing," what happens if the person who brings you all that happiness passes away? We are all mortal in this temporary existence we call being human, after all. The same thing goes for family. A tragic occurrence can change everything. And then where is all the happiness? It disappears, often condemning us to a meaningless life of unimaginable pain and seemingly endless suffering.

Of course, I'm not implying that we can avoid such pain or that we can somehow rise above suffering and feel no sadness. But if we give complete power to *anything* outside ourselves to make us happy, then we are at the complete mercy of circumstances to decide if we're happy or in endless suffering. If, on the other hand, the source of true happiness comes from the infinite well of love and joy within, then even though we may feel deep sadness and pain when something tragic occurs in our lives, we are not left in utter despair. A light still shines, and we can still live a life of meaning, fulfillment, and joy—no matter what happens in our lives.

This is the essence of the awakened life. It's a life wherein you're not the victim of circumstances. It's a life that is not blindly spent seeking pleasure and avoiding pain. It's a life of great soul evolution and progress along the path to our ultimate home. When we equate happiness with having our strongest desires met, no matter how noble those desires seem to be, we are trapped in the pleasure–pain principle. If I get what I want, then I feel happy. If I don't get what I want, then I suffer. But when, instead, we turn to the infinite source of joy within ourselves and draw from that, we break free from the trap of being emotionally enslaved by our life's circumstances. And that changes everything.

Now, all of a sudden, we are no longer relating to our romantic love partner as the source of our happiness (and therefore someone who can take it away), but rather sharing ourselves more fully and unconditionally. We are not demanding that another is the provider of our happiness and love, so we accept them as they are and give them the freedom to be themselves without conditions. This, in turn, changes the quality of the relationship, making it a more authentic exchange of love between two people rather than a conduit through which two people seek to get their needs met from each other in order to be happy. And true happiness and lasting fulfillment will not come from the latter.

The same principle applies to the relationships with our children. If we equate our entire source of happiness to our kids, then we will be enslaved with a paralyzing sense of fear our entire lives. What if, God forbid, something ever happened to them? Even though we may understand that we will see them again on the other side of the veil—as death is but a transition from one form of energy to another—we would destine ourselves to a life of living hell while still on this plane. But is this what life's about? Are we here to feel like helpless creatures in a big scary world, where any one of a number of difficult or tragic circumstances can leave us in emotional ruins and effectively end the meaning of our existence?

By now, you know my perspective on that. When I say connect to the true source of joy within you and draw from that infinite well, this is not simply a platitude or nice philosophy. As we have explored in depth from both a scientific and a spiritual perspective, it is the true nature of reality. We are Spirit having an experience called being human. Our true nature is not only divine but also immortal and infinite. We are literally connected with All That Is. And we don't have to have a direct experience of that on this plane to live our lives from this perspective. Instead, we can allow our understanding of the true nature of existence to become our bedrock of deep faith that cannot be disturbed. Once we have cultivated the kind of faith that is not blind but rather built from deep inner conviction, we can live life from that truth instead of getting caught on the hamster wheel of happiness—forever chasing something that we'll never get. Now we can live from a more centered place of assurance that all is ultimately well. Life will inevitably continue to challenge us, but even if, or when, we go through periods of discomfort and darkness, we'll find that the light that we truly are never dims. Living in this way evolves our consciousness and gets us ready to make the shift toward the fourth density, while simultaneously raising the collective consciousness of Earth.

TRAP #2: POSITIVE THINKING AND THE LAW OF ATTRACTION

When people turn to the subject of awakened living from a higher state of consciousness, they often start exploring how they can use the power of the mind to create a more positive reality. This type of self-development can be very helpful because it allows us to let go of victim-thinking and self-limiting beliefs. In fact, there's an entire movement behind the idea of positive thinking, as the hit movie *The Secret* set ablaze a worldwide interest in the law of attraction (the idea that you attract to you those life circumstances that reflect your most emotionally charged thoughts). And while I'm not suggesting that the law of attraction doesn't exist in some form, or that positive thinking can't have some great effects (I have used both extensively in life and business myself), it's worth being aware of the not-so-obvious hidden trap beneath their seemingly beautiful exterior.

When we come to understand some of the true nature of reality, such as the effect of thought on the seemingly physical world (which we saw to be true in the study of the 7,000 meditators in Chapter 2, among other scientific evidence), it can be a powerful thing. But only having *some* of the picture can also be a dangerous thing. And that's what tends to occur with devotees of positive thinking and the law of attraction. They have some of the picture, which is that our thoughts directly influence our physical reality. But what's missing is the *spiritual* reality of the universe and the true purpose of existence.

The issue with positive thinking and the law of attraction is that they turn our entire focus on getting what we desire and so can inadvertently bring us right back to the pleasure–pain trap. Instead of hoping and praying that we get what we want in life so that we can be happy, we turn to using our (incomplete) understanding of the true nature of reality and the power of our minds to bring us happiness. Different means, same end. And here we fall into another trap because we believe, "This will bring me the happiness that I seek." But the hidden writing on the wall here is "seek and do not find" because happiness can't be found outside us; it has to come from within.

This is also the meaning behind the famous inscription on the Temple of Apollo at Delphi: "Know thyself." It is not about knowing your strengths and weaknesses, which are just aspects of the personality of the physical self you think yourself to be. It is about knowing the true divine essence within yourself that brings true happiness and fulfillment. And this fulfillment can't be found in rearranging life's circumstances to meet your desires because if you're not connected to the true joy within, then changing the circumstances of life is like changing the furniture in a burning house. Sure, you have beautiful new furniture that you "love," but how does that really matter when your whole house is burning down?

But there's an even subtler and more insidious trap at play here. When we choose to use positive thinking and the law of attraction (through various techniques such as creative visualization), we often start actively resisting our negative thoughts. We now have great respect for the power of our thoughts to create our reality, and so naturally we want to block out negative thoughts. We are told that what we focus on and give our attention to will manifest, and this makes us not want to focus on the negativity and darkness within ourselves. But this is the biggest trap of all. And to understand why, we must remember the *whole* nature of reality and the ultimate purpose of our existence.

Remember that we are not here just to manifest our heart's every desire and get what we want. We are here (especially within the third-density plane of existence) to learn how to make the choice to love unconditionally within the very convincing illusion of separation. This is the challenging classroom in which we set out to learn what true unconditional love actually means. For if we remain completely connected to our Source in our natural divine and perfect state, then it would be easy to love. We can only understand the true meaning of love (which is what we *are*), and expand the essence of that love, by learning how to be loving *despite* every reason not to be. And these reasons not only extend to others who may upset us but also to *ourselves*.

If you think about it, we are often harshest with ourselves. We all want to think that we are good, kind, honest, and loving people, but when we fall short of these high standards (which can happen often), we tend to judge ourselves quite harshly. We might feel a deep sense of guilt or remorse and punish ourselves with unkind thoughts and negative emotions.

Now if we happen to be working on attracting something we desire by being very positive in our thoughts and emotions, then we can feel threatened when we find ourselves having negative thoughts and emotions. We start thinking that the negative thoughts and feelings will not only keep away what we desire, but also bring bad circumstances into our lives. And here is where the biggest trap of all is laid. We came into this physical incarnation to learn the lesson of how to choose to be unconditionally loving. One of the main ways we choose to learn it is by taking on a physical persona that is very imperfect. This is not who we truly are but rather a temporary vehicle for learning. And how can we use this vehicle for the deep learning it was meant to provide? We do it by continually forgiving and having compassion for the imperfection. For what is unconditional love but complete forgiveness and compassion—no matter what?

So you see, any darkness and negativity that you see in yourself is not to be shunned and judged as bad or sinful. When you do that, you are not actually getting rid of it, but simply repressing it into the subconscious mind. It's still there. You might feel better on the surface by pretending it's not, but that doesn't change anything. The idea, then, is not to try to get rid of it because it makes you feel like you're a bad person, but rather to remember that not only are you not a bad person, but also that *you're not even a person.* You are Spirit having an experience called being a person. And you chose this experience very specifically so you can understand love on a deeper level and expand the essence of what you are from this experience. You *chose* to incarnate as an imperfect human. This can be looked at as the more correct interpretation of the religious concept of the fall of man. You were never in a perfect state *as* a human in the Garden of Eden, falling from grace due to your inherent sinful self. Rather, you were (and still are beyond the illusion of space and time) in a perfect state as *Spirit*, and you chose to "fall" not because you were sinful, but rather to purposefully learn the lessons of unconditional love in the more challenging and fruitful environment of imperfection and seeming separation from love.

Looked at from this perspective, the negative and dark aspects of ourselves that we so often judge and hate can take on a new meaning. Now, instead of repressing them and not giving attention to them for fear of what that means about us, or for fear of what we'll attract, we can shine a loving light on them and bring all of that darkness to the surface without fear. And when we make what was previously unconscious conscious, it loses its power over us. Now we are no longer reacting automatically to our inner demons but rather *responding consciously,* and our response is acceptance, compassion, forgiveness, and love.

THE TRUE MESSAGE OF ALL RELIGIONS

The subject of truly unconditional acceptance and forgiveness can be difficult to accept if you were raised in a religious family and taught to believe heavily in sin and a judgmental Creator. But let's think about the true teachings behind the religion. The reality is that most religions teach the tenets of love and forgiveness. Jesus taught about forgiveness possibly more than any other teacher. He taught to forgive *no matter what,* and he acted as the ultimate example of that by forgiving even those who crucified him. He truly personified the meaning of unconditional forgiveness, and this often seems to be forgotten by those claiming to believe his message while judging and condemning others. Jesus' message was not "believe in me and you will be saved, even if you continue to judge yourself and others." His true *undistorted* message was "be like me, and you will be saved." That, I believe, is the true meaning behind the statement "I am the way, and the truth, and the light." It means that his thoughts and actions were showing the way, the truth, and the light.

And it wasn't only Jesus who displayed this way of being but so did other great prophets and masters from different time periods. And why will being like them save you? Not because you are inherently sinful and need saving but because "being saved" in this instance means learning the lessons you are here to learn and thereby ascending to a higher density plane of existence. We don't automatically ascend to the fourth-density plane of love with the arrival of the quantum leap in evolution, described in the previous chapter. If we have not sufficiently learned the lessons of love, then we will need to repeat a 25,960-year cycle of numerous more incarnations on third-density planets to learn the lesson sufficiently.

Of course, the subject of offering love and forgiveness naturally applies to others and not just to ourselves. Just as our job is not to be perfect, but rather to forgive our imperfections and therefore learn the only lesson we're here to learn, we can remember that no one else deserves anything but our compassion and forgiveness. No matter how bad or evil they seem to be, we can remind ourselves of who and what they truly are behind the illusion of their physical selves, and we can be thankful for the opportunity to learn our lesson of love that they are offering us.

However, if instead we choose to judge and condemn others, then all we are really doing is choosing to condemn ourselves.

Why? Well, as we have seen and repeated numerous times, there is only One interconnecting energy here seeming to be many. All we are really doing when we're relating to others is relating to other *selves*; relating to other aspects of the Infinite Creator that share their ultimate reality with each one of us. So, no matter what you see and how bad or evil or dark it seems, do not condemn it but forgive it. Even if you don't believe or accept anything I'm saying about the true nature of reality, what good does condemning it do? And if you're religious, is that what religion actually teaches you to do? Look at the wonderful infographic provided in Figure 8.1 (which has appeared in various places on the Internet) that shows the overriding message of nearly every major religion on earth.

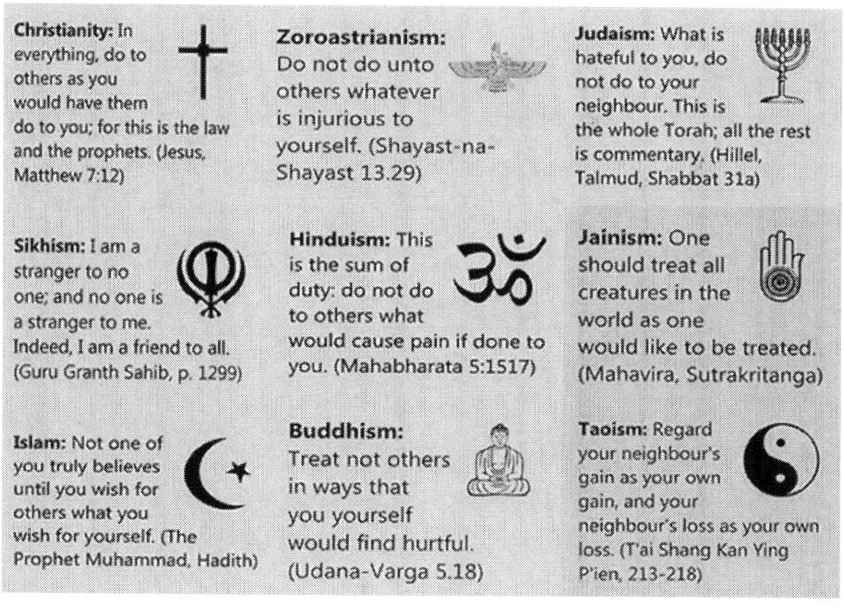

Christianity: In everything, do to others as you would have them do to you; for this is the law and the prophets. (Jesus, Matthew 7:12)

Zoroastrianism: Do not do unto others whatever is injurious to yourself. (Shayast-na-Shayast 13.29)

Judaism: What is hateful to you, do not to do your neighbour. This is the whole Torah; all the rest is commentary. (Hillel, Talmud, Shabbat 31a)

Sikhism: I am a stranger to no one; and no one is a stranger to me. Indeed, I am a friend to all. (Guru Granth Sahib, p. 1299)

Hinduism: This is the sum of duty: do not do to others what would cause pain if done to you. (Mahabharata 5:1517)

Jainism: One should treat all creatures in the world as one would like to be treated. (Mahavira, Sutrakritanga)

Islam: Not one of you truly believes until you wish for others what you wish for yourself. (The Prophet Muhammad, Hadith)

Buddhism: Treat not others in ways that you yourself would find hurtful. (Udana-Varga 5.18)

Taoism: Regard your neighbour's gain as your own gain, and your neighbour's loss as your own loss. (T'ai Shang Kan Ying P'ien, 213-218)

Figure 8.1 The true message of all religions

Somehow, it seems easy to forget that this is the real message of religion. We see many who profess to have faith in one religion or another getting caught up in doing the exact opposite—judging and condemning those of different beliefs. And if you aren't religious and think you're above all of this judging, then honestly ask yourself if you don't secretly harbor judgment and condemnation for those who have such opposing beliefs.

Really ask yourself, am I actually following the tenets of my religious or spiritual path? Or am I just paying lip service to it but actually doing the exact opposite? And no matter what seemingly wrong and evil actions others around you and in the world are doing, doesn't it make more sense to forgive than to condemn in light of your newfound understanding of the true nature of reality? If you can see the darkness inside yourself and, instead of judging and resisting it, look at the human you are with compassion and forgiveness, you can do that with others too. Everyone here, like you, is actually Spirit in temporary, imperfect human form, looking to learn the lessons of love. The only thing that separates any of us is not how good or evil we are but how connected we are with our true Self behind the illusion of separation. The reality is that everyone is connected, and we can never lose that connection, but we can forget it, block it, or be completely unaware that it is there.

Does that mean these souls, who are stuck in the illusion of separation and all the fear that it entails, deserve our condemnation? Or do they deserve our compassion instead? Think of everyone you hate—whether it's a person, country, or race, and regardless of the worldly justification for your hate and anger—and ask yourself these questions in light of everything discussed here and see if you don't come to the conclusion that it is compassion that is warranted in every instance, not judgment and condemnation. Even if they cause great pain and harm to others, they are in great pain in their soul, feeling completely disconnected from and abandoned by their Source.

THE ESSENCE OF COMPASSION AND FORGIVENESS

Now please don't make the mistake of thinking that compassion and forgiveness mean letting people commit crimes and atrocities without consequences. This is not at all what I'm saying. We need to differentiate between the physical and spiritual levels. On the physical level, if someone is perpetrating a crime, they need to be punished. If a country is oppressing others, its government needs to be sanctioned and overthrown. But these actions can be taken while continuing to hold compassion and forgiveness in our hearts to the best of our ability. That is what determines our progress and evolution of consciousness on the spiritual level.

In the same way, if someone cheats you in business, it is absolutely *not* unspiritual to sue them, if that's what's required. You can be deeply spiritual and loving, and still take this person to court. What's of true importance is your internal attitude. Are you taking them to court while thinking of them as an evil person, and feeling anger and hatred toward them? Or are you taking them to court knowing that, even though they have wronged you on the physical level, on the spiritual level they are one with you? The latter perspective allows you to feel compassion for the human they are, seeing them as one who has temporarily lost awareness of their connection to the Source and operating from separation consciousness, while the former keeps you trapped in separation consciousness.

So many people make the wrong assumption, especially in new-age spirituality, that being a spiritual, loving person equals being a walkover and not seeking justice in the world. This stems simply from a lack of understanding of the difference between the physical and spiritual planes. We cannot have an orderly physical world without a certain amount of laws and justice. And while we are incarnated on the physical plane, we need to respect and honor the physical aspect.

Therefore the best advice is to simply be "normal." Normal people take action to defend themselves. If someone comes at you with a knife, that is not the time to look at them and see Oneness and the unconditional love of their true Spirit Self. That is the time to run or even fight back in self-defense. But after acting in the appropriate way on the physical front, try not to harbor resentment and hatred toward your attacker, but see them as someone who has come to teach you how to love despite how difficult it may be. That is the true meaning of being a spiritual person who is living an awakened life, dedicated to evolving their consciousness and fulfilling their deeper purpose. Honor the illusion and its rules, but be aware of what is beyond it.

And so, to conclude and bring everything together, when you let go of attachment to your desires—knowing they won't bring true fulfillment—and accept (even embrace) the negative or dark aspects of yourself and others, then you can go through life having what you want while also living out your deeper purpose and evolving your consciousness to make the shift to a higher plane of existence.

Some people assume that living out your life's true purpose necessitates giving up all desires, especially on the material front, and living the life of a monk. The reality is that we're not here to shun the physical but to use it to learn the deeper lessons of love. And ironically enough, we are often able to manifest our desires with even greater ease when we let go of attachments and embrace the darkness we see within and without. That's because the subconscious mind is much more powerful than the conscious mind in dictating our reality. So while you may be thinking positive thoughts on the conscious level, if you resist the dark and negative aspects of yourself—and the thoughts that come with it— then your subconscious will be dictating your reality, regardless of whether you're using positive thinking or not. But when we bring our darker aspects to the light of consciousness, they are transmuted and no longer hold a secret power over us, and that's when, ironically, we end up receiving what we desire—and without all the struggle and suffering that comes with giving it power over us and becoming a slave to its screaming demands.

This advice extends not only to all those who are devout followers of positive thinking and the law of attraction but also to those who subscribe to new-age spirituality, which tends to affirm only the light and completely ignores the darkness or evil. As Carl Jung so eloquently stated, "One does not become enlightened by imagining figures of light, but by making the darkness conscious."

And with that said, in the next chapter we'll turn to how to bring all of this together to live an awakened life based on *true spirituality*, which not only evolves your consciousness toward higher states of existence, but will bring you true peace and deep fulfillment along the way.

AWAKENING PRACTICES

The following practices can be done any time. I recommend you spend at least 5–10 minutes on each one, staying with it for as long as you'd like. If you resonate deeply with one or more, you might choose to make it a daily practice. Each awakening practice was created to help you apply the knowledge you're learning, and so raise your consciousness and deepen your connection to the truth of your being.

Before starting each practice, silence your phone and try to make sure that you won't be disturbed. Sit or lie down in a comfortable position, close your eyes, and gently begin.

Ultimate Freedom

- This practice will help you find freedom from your attachments and desires. Each time you use it, you'll move further away from being a slave to their dictates—forever chasing pleasure and avoiding pain—to resting in the perfect presence that you are and drawing joy from the infinite well within.

- Take several deep breaths, relaxing with each one, and then let your breathing return to its normal rhythm.

- Begin to think of all your strong attachments in life. Think about your attachment to your family, children, spouse, partner, money, material possessions, and anything else that comes to mind.

- Now, taking each one in turn, fully welcome and embrace that attachment. This is very counterintuitive because our instinct is to push it away, or try to get rid of it, in order to let go of attachment to it. But the exact opposite is true. What you resist persists, and it's in gentle, nonjudgmental

158

welcoming that true release occurs. Of course a part of you will naturally resist this process, especially when it comes to releasing the attachment to a child or partner. But here it must be understood that releasing attachment is not letting go of caring. To the contrary, it's only when you release your attachment that you can truly love selflessly and unconditionally, because that love will no longer be distorted by fear.

- After you're done welcoming and embracing your attachments, repeat the same process with your strongest desires. One by one, fully welcome and embrace them without judgment. Notice the release and spaciousness that comes with this acceptance. If you find it hard to welcome, you can try gently saying "it's OK" and remember that you are loved no matter what you feel.

- Relax and enjoy the experience of freedom.

EMBRACING THE DARKNESS

This practice helps you bring the light of consciousness to those aspects of yourself that you may currently keep buried in your subconscious. The more you fearlessly look at the darkness and let go of your resistance to it, the more you'll experience your true Self, and along with it deep peace and joy.

- Take several deep breaths, relaxing with each one, and then let your breathing return to its normal rhythm.

- Now bring into your awareness those aspects of yourself that you find negative or dark. It could be a personality trait that you think is "bad," something that you feel guilty about, or thoughts or emotions that you find shameful or even outright evil.

- Whatever it is, one by one, hold it in your awareness and let the limitless spring of love from your heart fully embrace it. If this seems hard to do, and you find your judgment of it is so strong that you can't accept and embrace it, remember that from the Infinite Creator's perspective, everything is valid and equal because it is all part of Its One Self and Its desire to experience Itself. So nothing that you think, feel, or do is "bad" or "wrong" from the ultimate sense beyond the illusion. Your whole purpose here is to learn how to love unconditionally, and your perceived shameful aspects of self are the perfect tool to help you do that. In truth you are perfect and any perceived darkness is not what or who you truly are. So welcome the darkness. Don't judge it, and don't be afraid of it. Embrace it, and allow it to dissolve in the light of love.

- To help you do that, you can say to yourself "I am unconditionally loved by creation itself, and nothing that I think or do can change that. The darkness I see within is not a defect, but my teacher, to which I am grateful."

- Rest in this fearless appreciation for as long as you like.

EMBODYING COMPASSION

We're often blinded by our anger and find it hard to find compassion for someone who has caused us pain. This practice allows you to look at others through a powerful new lens, seeing beyond their hurtful words and actions to the truth that opens the door to real compassion and kindness.

- Take several deep breaths, relaxing with each one, and then let your breathing return to its normal rhythm.

- Think of someone you dislike, or someone you love who has hurt you. Let the pain or hatred come up, but don't get stuck in a mental story that justifies your irritation, hurt, or anger. Instead, look beyond appearances and try to see the pain inside that person.

- Acknowledge that no one acts in a hurtful way without

being in deep pain. The hurtful actions, while seemingly targeted at you, are not really about you. Instead, they are a projection of the unbearable pain that person is feeling within. And even if the pain is not apparent to you, and you see no reason why they should be in pain, realize that this is not an emotional pain that is related to present circumstances. Each of us in the third- density plane of existence has suffered much throughout many lifetimes, and we all carry an immense amount of pain inside. This is the pain—common to you and everyone else—that you need to perceive. So see the hurt, small child within that person and have compassion. No matter what they've done to hurt you, know it wasn't truly purposeful. They are hurting and they need your compassion. See them not as they are, but as their small child self, lashing out because it is in pain and feeling fear.

- To help you do that, you can imagine kneeling down to this little child and telling them that it's OK. That you know they're in pain and aren't purposefully trying to hurt you, and you're here for them. Give that small child a hug and feel your compassion healing them. Whether you know it or not, both of you are being deeply healed in that holy moment.

CHAPTER 9

LIVING THE
AWAKENED LIFE

"Where the spirit does not work
with the hand, there is no art."

– Leonardo Da Vinci

While it's important to understand the nature of reality on an intellectual level, it's in the daily living of these principles that true spirituality is experienced, and lasting happiness and fulfillment found. We have to be careful not to practice a sort of spiritual arrogance, where we unconsciously (or even consciously) believe we are superior to others because we are "more spiritual." As you'll know by now this is a consciousness of separation rather than unity.

Living a truly spiritual and awakened life is not just about praying and meditating and performing rituals. The essence of the path is *living* it on a daily basis. That's the only thing that is actually worth anything in the end. If all the reading and praying and meditating doesn't lead us to become more kind, loving, nonjudgmental, and forgiving, then what good has it really done?

What have we really learned?

And so our goal now is to create a practical framework from all these principles, so that we can learn what we're really here to learn. The illusion can seem so convincing on this third-density plane of existence that it can often be quite difficult to practice being loving and forgiving consistently. So the first step in creating a practical framework is to gain a greater understanding of the mechanics behind the illusion of separation, and in doing so become better equipped to handle its challenges.

THE MULTIDIMENSIONAL ASPECT OF SELF

If you're like most people, you believe you are your body. You believe you *are* the human who was born into this world and that you *are* your name, your personality, and your personal history. But while this may be an aspect of you, it is but a tiny, temporary part of who and what you truly are. In reality, you are a vast, multidimensional being who exists simultaneously on many levels. Once you accept that time and space are purposeful illusions and nothing more, then you realize that "you" can simultaneously exist in many different times and places, including being beyond *all* time and space.

As Dr. Michael Newton's research showed,[17-18] each of us has an individuated "separate" soul, but this soul is not completely "in" the physical body. Rather, the soul gives part of its energy to incarnate into the physical, but it still exists in the nonphysical realm at the same time. While we are in human form, however, we are not conscious of our "other" existence. And as *The Law of One* teachings state, at the sixth-density plane of existence and higher, we go beyond being an individual soul with a separate identity and merge into a state of oneness that is incredibly more

164

expansive and completely beyond physical limits. But if this state exists in a much higher density that we are evolving toward over a very long period of time, and we only reach it in our distant future as souls, then how could that be who we truly are in essence *now*?

This brings us to one of the most important principles that can help us live life in human form. Namely, modern science has shown us that time is an illusion, so that the "you" without physical limits that is made of pure unending love and joy (which your soul is evolving toward in the distant future) exists in that state *now*. There is only *now*. What we perceive of as past, present, and future are actually coordinates in a three-dimensional structure of time, and regardless of the coordinate you choose, it's still *now* there. Only the *now* exists.

The most helpful way I've found to understand this often-confusing subject is to think of it from a top-down model. Instead of just thinking of yourself as a human or a soul evolving its way toward higher and higher densities, think of yourself as a vast, limitless being who is already in a state of perfection and unconditional love at the highest planes of existence, looking to expand yourself infinitely by experiencing seeming individuation and separation (i.e., becoming individual souls) and then coming back home to yourself with an expanded and deeper sense of self.

Remaining in a state of pure love, while beautiful, wouldn't provide us with an opportunity to expand that love that we are and fully understand it. Creating the illusion of separation, however, provides us with ample opportunities to learn to express love in the most challenging of circumstances. So experiencing the difficulties of being unconditionally loving serves to expand the love that we are in the higher plane of existence and to understand ourselves more deeply. As this experience is occurring, however, on *this* level, it's easy to "forget" our true essence and instead believe we are an individual soul working their way up the ladder of spiritual evolution, striving for expansion and perfection. The ultimate truth is that both (and all) states exist now.

The beautiful insight that is gleaned from all of this is that you already *are* that which you have always longed to become. It's just that, at this level, you have no direct constant access to it and you have to go through the steps toward it.

So when does it end? It never ends. When we say "Infinite Creator," the word *infinite* is very literal. This is a cyclical process of expansion that is literally endless. As one cycle comes to completion, the universe is "completed" and another is born to allow for more experience and expansion.

This process itself is also nonlinear, as scientists are now realizing the very real possibility that countless parallel universes exist simultaneously, each going through its own cycle of expansion and completion in a different way.[48] Reality, as it turns out, is far different from what we thought. Not only is it holographic but also nonlinear and multidimensional. The "you" who you think you are is really but a tiny fraction of all that you actually are. You are a limitless being that has "split itself" multidimensionally, and you're now consciously experiencing one small part of yourself on this level.

A STORY OF TWO SELVES

Understanding our true nature in this way can help us navigate life, especially if we simplify and not get too lost in the multidimensional aspect of things. To do that, try thinking of yourself more simply in two ways: physical self and Spirit Self.

The physical self is the human who you think yourself to be with its individual soul, and the Spirit Self is the limitless nonphysical being that exists in the seventh-density plane of existence. It is your Spirit Self that expands (how the limitless can expand is the profound mystery of creation) from the experiences of your physical self. Your physical self is the vehicle; your Spirit Self the driver. I have created the following diagram (see figure 9.1) to help you visualize yourself existing on two planes simultaneously (this is only a useful simplification; in truth we are multidimensional beings). As you see, your Spirit Self completely encompasses your physical self. The physical self is simply the conduit through which the Spirit Self (your true Self) experiences.

Figure 9.1 Two aspects of the self

The thing to understand is that all our troubles occur when our physical self thinks that it is all of who we are and it feels alone in a big, scary universe. This is the essence of separation consciousness. The physical self feels separate from its Source. And because it feels so small and alone and fears for its existence, it feels a massive desire to *control* its life and destiny. In fact, when the physical self doesn't connect to the Spirit Self, everything we think and do is, consciously or unconsciously, driven by *fear*.

You might be thinking that there are many people in this world who are not aware of the higher Spirit Self but are still good and loving, and aren't dictated by fear. That's definitely true, but just because we're not all aware of the Spirit Self on a conscious level doesn't mean that we aren't subconsciously drawing inspiration from it. When we are, that's when we're truly *unselfishly* loving. But it's also true that what passes for goodness and love in this world is often nothing more than disguised fear. For instance, most romantic relationships are not based on real love but rather on fear masquerading as love. It is the fear that "I am not enough" and therefore need the love of another person to feel complete. And the acts that seem loving are often (unconsciously) acts that are actually seeking approval from the other person.

We know this to be true by how we feel when we do something loving for a loved one and they don't acknowledge it or respond favorably. Anger and hurt are the usual feelings that arise. But if we're simply performing a loving act for the sake of love itself, and not unconsciously seeking approval, then why would we feel angry and hurt if the act is not acknowledged or reciprocated? Only if the act is triggered from an unconscious fear that "I am not enough" will it cause such feelings to arise, because the lack of acknowledgement and reciprocation seems to confirm the very fear that gave rise to the act.

This fear extends to every area of our lives, and deep unconscious fear and a seeking of approval, control, or personal security will often drive even the seemingly kindest acts. But (and this is a big but), *none of this* is cause for judgment. If you remember that on one level you are already whole and complete, and you chose to incarnate into human form simply to expand the fullness, quality, and depth of that which you already are, then you can gain a tremendous amount of compassion for the human aspect of the total you, which thinks it is alone and lives in fear. And gaining this *unconditional* love and compassion is your life's true ultimate purpose!

And so, here is what I have found to be tremendously helpful in my own life. Live life with the strong faith and belief that who you are is far greater than this human you believe yourself to be. Understand, moreover, that there is a grand purpose to your human life and that your Spirit Self planned this life in such a way as to provide the best lessons for practicing fearless, unselfish love in highly challenging conditions. Instead of feeling victimized by a big, bad world, realize that your life is your classroom, and Earth is no kindergarten class. It is a university-level education that you are enrolled in here. Be thankful for that and at the same time feel compassion for this human who is often unaware of the bigger picture and its grander purpose. Remind yourself every single day that *everything* that happens to you happens for your own good in the ultimate sense. Your Spirit Self knows what is needed for the evolution of your soul and plans everything, no matter how painful or tragic it seems.

You planned it all. You are the writer of this play. You are also its director, the actor, and the audience. It's only when you get caught up in the role of the actor and forget that it's just a role that life seems to be scary and fear becomes warranted. But how much fear would you feel, if you knew that everything that will *ever* happen to you, good and bad, is gently planned by a greater part of yourself that knows what is ultimately best for you and knows what you need to learn on a soul level? How much would you resist the events of your life then?

And so, to live a truly awakened life and to find deep meaning and purpose, look at your entire life as what it rightfully is: a curriculum. Your life, and everything that happens in it, is your curriculum in this university-level education. Moreover, you customized the entire curriculum for yourself, knowing exactly what you needed to work on and learn. And this curriculum does not only show up when one of life's major challenges or tragedies arise. *Every single moment of every single day of your entire life is part of the curriculum.* Why? Because each and every moment you have the choice of whether you're going to *unconsciously react* to life's circumstances and triggers or if you'll *consciously respond.* The difference is that the former is dictated by fear, while the latter is inspired by love.

CONNECTING TO THE SPIRIT SELF

When we live life under the dictates of the physical self, without consistent conscious connection with our higher Spirit Self, we go through life reenacting a conditioned set of unconscious responses. Someone cuts us off in traffic, and anger erupts and we start swearing. Someone says something unkind, and we instantly feel a surge of defensiveness and lash out in retaliation. We make a mistake on an important project, and we get frustrated and start beating ourselves up internally.

Most of us go through the majority of our lives this way,

thinking that we are free while never realizing that we are nothing but slaves to life's triggers and our conditioned, unconscious reactions. We are slaves because we are not *choosing* how to respond to any given set of stimuli but rather reacting without choice. Later on we might rationalize how "that asshole cut me off" and he deserved to be yelled at, but that is only an after-the-fact rationalization. In the moment, we were slaves to our habitual conditioning and didn't realize we had a choice. We didn't realize that, for instance, we could have connected to our Spirit Self and chosen to see the other driver as a brother or sister who is also living life in fear and therefore have compassion for them. We could have chosen to remember the interconnected nature of reality and the ultimate Oneness behind the illusion of separation and realize that, in the ultimate sense, that person *is our Self.* Or if that is too much of a stretch for us to believe right now, we could have simply remembered that our life is a curriculum and that this person is providing us with a wonderful opportunity to be loving and forgiving, and in truth, they deserve not condemnation but *gratitude.*

When we go through life absorbed by the acting role that we call our physical self and remain oblivious to our larger nature and reality as Spirit, none of these more skillful choices of conscious response are available to us. We get angry and swear and throw a fit. We then often remain in this negative energy and let it influence our interactions with those closest to us. We may feel righteous in our bad mood, but then often that righteousness turns to guilt, and we feel bad for how we've been acting. Then we start punishing ourselves internally, which does nothing but solidify the unconscious patterns of reaction that ensure that the vicious cycle is kept alive and we act the exact same way the next time something like this happens.

This is how most people lead their lives on a daily basis, to one degree or another. And that's why most people are deeply unhappy and unfulfilled beneath the surface, no matter how cheerful their countenances may be. They are not practicing being truly loving. They are unconsciously leading their lives as slaves of their physical selves, and therefore life lacks true meaning. It becomes nothing more than a cycle of waking up, going through the daily routine, and falling asleep, only to repeat it all the next day, devoid of any real meaning and true spiritual evolution. Even when life circumstances change on the outside and everything seems great and better than ever, internally things remain the same. No true growth in consciousness has occurred.

But this doesn't have to be the case. What your soul yearns for more than anything else is that connection with its true Spirit essence. When you find that connection and practice establishing it on a daily basis, it grows stronger and stronger and you become more and more skillful in reaching for it at that very moment when you would have previously reacted unconsciously. Now you find that you notice the feelings arising, and these act as an alert that an unconscious pattern has been triggered. Now, instead of slavishly reacting to it, you can choose to respond more lovingly in a conscious way.

To help you do that, let's delve into the specifics of how to actually do this on a practical basis.

The Skillful Practice of Unconditional Love

One of the most common traps on the awakening or consciousness evolution path, and one I have fallen into on many occasions, is thinking that we have to be perfect. When we become awakened to the true nature of reality, we feel a genuine desire to be kind and loving to everyone and everything. This makes us feel that it is unacceptable to feel the so-called negative emotions of anger, hatred, jealousy, fear, greed, lust, pride, and so on. In doing so, we give birth to a strong desire to get rid of all of them so that we can be loving and kind all the time. We think that if we are feeling them, then we are no longer being spiritual and that we need to get rid of them to get back to being spiritual. And if we (as we always end up doing) become angry, fearful, jealous, or prideful, then we feel like we have failed and a tremendous amount of guilt and self-judgment takes hold.

Although being kind and loving all the time to everyone and everything is a very noble desire, what is most often missed among everyone and everything that we want to be kind to, is *ourselves*. We forget to be kind, loving, and compassionate with ourselves. We forget that the physical self was not meant to be perfect, nor could it ever be on this plane of existence, and as such, it need not be judged for its lack of perfection. More importantly, we forget that just as our whole lives are a curriculum for practicing forgiveness and compassion, so is our *physical self* its own purposeful curriculum.

Think about it. The physical self is limited by its very nature. It is limited by the senses and cannot perceive the vast majority of what actually exists all around it. It is limited by the density of its energy, giving it distinct physical boundaries and an absolute sense of separation from its environment. It is limited in its intelligence and how much it can actually know about any given situation. It is limited in its perception of time and true cause and effect. It is limited by the fact that its consciousness is highly fragmented and compartmentalized into a conscious, subconscious, and unconscious, and it often has no idea how to access anything beyond the conscious. It is also limited from the sense that it is programmed, *by its very nature*, to produce emotions, some of which are uncomfortable.

Given all of these limitations, which are *by design*, it would make sense that they are meant to be used for learning purposes instead of being shunned as something undesirable. Remember, if you had already learned the lessons you needed to, then you would not be incarnated in human form in the third density with all of these limitations to begin with. So the limitations are not bad, and they are not to be judged. They are purposeful learning mechanisms.

For instance, if you have an anger problem, then you likely hate the fact that you get angry so much and probably even feel a lot of shame around it. I know I've personally dealt with this issue throughout my life. Thankfully, I never had the issue of expressing my anger physically and hurting others, but lashing out emotionally toward others and myself has been something I've dealt with since I was young. For the longest time, I felt a tremendous amount of shame because I didn't want to be angry; I wanted to be kind and loving instead. This shame intensified when I became more spiritually aware because it felt like such a contradiction to understand all of these grand truths about reality and yet still get so angry on a regular basis. Internally, it felt like hypocrisy. But then it all finally hit me, and I suddenly understood.

I now understand that anger is not some weakness or inadequacy that I should judge and feel bad about. Looked at from the higher perspective, my Spirit Self knew what I needed to learn in this life. It knew that a most challenging lesson would be to choose a body with a genetic makeup that is predisposed to having a personality that would become excessively angry, because it would require a lot of compassion and self-love to accept this angry self and not feel shame or judgment toward it.

From another perspective, I also understood my anger to be due to not receiving unconditional love in my childhood. This is *not* because my parents were unloving. On the contrary, I have wonderful and very loving parents. But the reality is that *none of us* received unconditional love as children because we were all raised by parents who were lost in the role of their physical selves and therefore unconsciously acting out of fear rather than true love much of the time. In addition to this, physical reality, by its very nature, cannot be unconditionally supportive.

Parents cannot possibly respond to every single need of a child instantaneously and, on an emotional level, each unmet need results in strong emotions becoming trapped in the very cellular structure of the growing child. When this is also added to the fact that we all come into each incarnation with the soul memory of many previous lifetimes and all the pain and suffering that they entailed, it's not surprising that anger is a common denominator among so many people. And if it's not anger, then it's some other limiting emotion that we judge as bad and shameful, and want so desperately to get rid of.

But what does it truly mean to be unconditionally loving? It does *not* mean that we are perfect in being loving toward everyone and everything because that is impossible on this plane of existence; and if we had the ability to do that, then we would not be in this plane with this particular classroom and set of lessons to begin with. This is very important to understand. What it *does* mean is that we genuinely and sincerely attempt to be loving to everyone and everything, and we continually forgive and find compassion for all the times that we can't do this. This is the only thing that extends the unconditional love to ourselves. Without this, we will be trying (and inevitably failing many times) to be loving to everyone, but we will be cruel and judgmental toward ourselves. And in this way, we're not truly learning the lesson of unconditional love.

Don't think that you are being spiritual only when you are being kind and loving and unspiritual when you are experiencing and expressing negative emotions. The true lesson of unconditional love is to understand the paradox that your physical self was never meant to be able to express love unconditionally and to love and accept it, nonetheless. That is what unconditional means: to see the limitations of self and *still* forgive and accept that self unconditionally. This doesn't mean that I'm advocating acting immorally and then just forgiving and accepting it. Please don't make this wrong assumption. I mean that you strive to be as loving, kind, honest, and forgiving as possible, and when you inevitably fail due to your humanness (which will happen many times each day if you watch yourself with awareness), you have compassion for your human self and forgive it completely. *That* is the meaning of unconditional love on this third-density plane that we are here to learn. Seeking perfection in how you act toward others while ignoring the compassion toward self is not what you're here to learn.

Make no mistake, this is a very tricky lesson to learn, and it takes a lot of practice and much self-awareness. The way to do it is to go about your day not so absorbed in the events of life but rather watching your feelings with awareness, even in the midst of all the busyness of life. When something seems to trigger you into an unconscious pattern of acting in an unkind manner, catch the rising emotion in the moment as quickly as possible and *don't* judge yourself for it. Realize that it is normal and a valid part of being human. Remind yourself that being a spiritual person and living an awakened life does not mean that you won't have negative thoughts and feelings. Rather, simply feel the feeling fully without judgment. Let it be there. And realize that it's just a feeling. It, in itself, is *not* a problem.

The problem arises only when we let that feeling unconsciously trigger a reaction. And even then, if you don't catch it in time and go into reaction mode, then the moment you realize that this happened, have compassion for yourself and forgive completely. You might like to ask yourself, "How would love respond?" Would unconditional love scold you and tell you, "You shouldn't have acted like that"? Or would it simply say, "It's OK." What else could unconditional love say other than "It's OK"?

Indeed, it is OK. It's always OK. You are simply learning. And even if you hurt another person, beating yourself up doesn't change anything. In fact, it does nothing more than keep the guilt alive that then, as Freud showed us, gets unconsciously projected onto others and causes nothing more than the repetition of the same pattern over and over.[49] But when you find compassion for this human who you experience yourself to be, then the chain is broken. You no longer get stuck in guilt, and you no longer project that guilt onto others and find fault in them to keep the negative cycle alive. So as counterintuitive as it may be, forgiving yourself, even when you hurt others, *does not* condone the act or give you permission to do it again but rather releases the guilt that would keep the whole cycle intact, therefore truly moving you in the right direction.

And what about those times when you do catch the emotion before you react unconsciously (which will happen more and more as you practice daily)? You realize that it is simply an emotion, it is valid, and has a right to be there. Even the most negative of emotions that you may judge to be bad because you think of yourself as a good and spiritual person are *valid*. They are simply arising in the moment and as such have validity. This doesn't mean that you get sucked into the story they're telling you. When we do that, we go from the direct experience of emotions (which sets them free) to a mental story about what those emotions mean. That's the trap. If someone wrongs you and you experience anger rising, then experiencing the anger with awareness in the moment doesn't have any bad consequences. In fact, it allows the anger to express itself and dissipate. The anger stays only when you start telling yourself a story about why you're justified to feel angry with that person. Now it's no longer a natural temporary emotion but rather a mental story that has taken on a life of its own and fuels a whole slew of negative emotions from which you have no escape.

WELCOMING WHAT IS

The reality is that there is another option apart from outwardly expressing and inwardly repressing emotion. Welcoming the emotion and feeling it fully without outwardly expressing it (shouting, swearing, fighting, etc.) or internally suppressing it (burying it in your heart or ignoring it) is the way to experience strong emotions without giving them control over our lives. Outwardly expressing and internally repressing keep us in slave mode. We either react without thinking or we hold it in until one day it all blows up when it becomes too much to bear inside. To be truly free, we must *feel* our emotions with full acceptance. Willingly embrace them no matter how uncomfortable. What you'll find is that they quickly dissolve. Why? Because embracing and fully accepting them is an act of unconditional love, and darkness dissolves in the light of love.

And this brings me to the final concept I want to share here, which is that it is not what happens in our life—nor the emotions we experience—that is ever a problem, but our *resistance* to them. Quite simply, as Carl Jung told us, what we resist persists. When we learn to welcome everything that happens in life, and to welcome all our emotions, we learn what true freedom is. We understand that life truly is not about manipulating and controlling circumstances to fit our desires but rather about surrendering and fearlessly accepting whatever arises in the moment, whether that is a seemingly negative or positive event or emotion. It is this equanimity toward life (both externally and internally) that is true freedom. Then we are no longer this small physical self struggling to have its needs met, fearful that it won't get its way. Rather, we go through the human experience in the understanding that it is a deeply meaningful classroom designed by none other than our larger aspect of Self for our own benefit. And in this light, our greatest enemy is our greatest teacher, to whom we should be very thankful.

Of course, I'm not implying that any of this is easy to do. I often still find it difficult too. It's all too easy to get sucked back into the busyness of life and to forget about of all of this "deeper spiritual stuff." And yet, as surely as the breath comes to fill your lungs again, so too will the call of your heart come again to remind you of what truly matters in your life. And when that happens, you remember, "It's OK." It has always been OK. You are loved beyond measure, and everything that happens is happening for your own ultimate good. So relax. Relax, and learn the beautiful lessons of love.

AWAKENING PRACTICES

The following practices can be done any time. I recommend you spend at least 5–10 minutes on each one, staying with it for as long as you'd like. If you resonate deeply with one or more, you might choose to make it a daily practice. Each awakening practice was created to help you apply the knowledge you're learning, and so raise your consciousness and deepen your connection to the truth of your being.

Before starting each practice, silence your phone and try to make sure that you won't be disturbed. Sit or lie down in a comfortable position, close your eyes, and gently begin.

EMBRACED BY THE SELF

This practice will help you connect to your Spirit Self and feel the deep love that characterizes it. The more you use it, the more you'll be able to find that connection during the busy and difficult moments of life, giving you stillness in the middle of the storm.

- Take several deep breaths, relaxing with each one, and then let your breathing return to its normal rhythm.

- Visualize your Spirit Self in the most meaningful way to you. You could think of it as a great white light above you, or a gentle invisible presence within and around you, or give it your own unique identification. Whichever way the Spirit Self appears to you (and even if you can't conjure up any image), the important part is to feel. Feel love flowing from it to you. There is no limit to this love; it is an endless river. Bathe in it. Let it wash over you completely, all the while realizing that it is you embracing yourself.

- Allow the greater aspect that is your Spirit Self, which is boundless in its love, to embrace the physical self you think yourself to be. Allow the physical self's burdens to dissolve completely in this love. Feel the compassion that your Spirit Self has for all the limitations that your human self has to deal with. Notice the nonjudgment and unconditional acceptance.

- Rest in that and hold this beautiful connection as long as you desire.

ETERNAL PRESENCE

We tend to go through life living in the past or the future, completely resistant or oblivious to the present moment. This practice will help you connect with the eternal now, becoming present to what is happening within you in each moment, and experiencing a sense of peace regardless of what's going on in your life or the world.

- Take several deep breaths, relaxing with each one, and then let your breathing return to its normal rhythm.

- Start to feel the physical sensations of your body. Feel the chair or bed against you. Feel any tingling in your extremities. Focus on each part of the body in turn, gently flowing from one to the other. Then experience them all at once. Be with that awareness. If there is pain or discomfort, be with it without resistance. Allow it to be there and gently welcome it.

- Now notice any emotions you are feeling. Let them be there. Just be with them and invite them to do whatever they'd like to do. They are a part of your energy and they have every right to be there, even if they happen to be uncomfortable or painful. They are just as valid as the positive emotions.

- Stay with the feelings in a state of acceptance, being the silent eternal observer, and experiencing this heightened state of awareness for as long as you like.

THE INNER CHILD

No matter how loving our parents were, each of us has an inner child that never received the unconditional love it needed. This practice allows you to re-parent that child that still exists within you energetically—healing old wounds and clearing the way for the experience of lasting peace and fulfillment.

- Take several deep breaths, relaxing with each one, and then let your breathing return to its normal rhythm.

- Start by connecting to your heart and feel the presence of love. Let it grow and expand. Now visualize your child self, at any age below seven years that feels right to you. Tell your child self that although you've abandoned him or her for so long, you're sorry and you're here now. You didn't know any better, but now you're ready to give the unconditional love that they needed.

- Seeing the child clearly, kneel down and give them a warm loving embrace. Speak to your child self sincerely, and let whatever words want to flow to do so. Then ask your child self what he or she needs from you to know that they're safe and loved. Give them what is needed and make the commitment to be there for them each day in whatever way you're needed, if only for a few moments.

- Let your child self know that you will slowly gain their trust again and consistently give all that they require from now on.

RADICAL FORGIVENESS

Forgiving others who have hurt us is often one of the most difficult things for us. This practice gives you a powerful process to reach true forgiveness. By drawing on the true nature of reality, it allows you to look at the whole idea of forgiveness in a new light, making it easier to release the anger and resentment you hold within.

- Take several deep breaths, relaxing with each one, and then let your breathing return to its normal rhythm.

- Start by thinking of someone you harbor resentment and anger toward. Feel those feelings, but before you get stuck in the mental story of how they wronged you and why your feelings are so justified, see that person as you in another form. They may seem like a completely separate person, and on this level of physical illusion they are, but beyond the illusion they're not only one with you—they *are* you. Remember, there's only One of us really here appearing to be many. We are all aspects of the One Infinite Creator, and every other aspect is really us in another illusory form. You are always looking in the mirror when you interact with anyone.

- Now ask yourself, "Would I offer myself hate or love?"

- Bestow that love on this seeming other. Let it pour forth from you to them keeping in mind you are the one receiving this love. For in a universe where all is truly One, what is the difference between giving and receiving?

CHAPTER 10

EMBRACED BY
THE INFINITE

"You are not a drop in the ocean.
You are the entire ocean in a drop."

– RUMI

Throughout Part II, we have been exploring the Spirit Self and the different densities that make up the structure of existence, including the highest densities in which this limitless Spirit resides. Although no "proof" can be given for either of these things, I didn't write about these subjects merely from a theoretical perspective. On the contrary, I have had the most profound blessing of directly experiencing a glimpse of this higher reality and therefore *know*, beyond mere belief, it exists. And so I would like to conclude by sharing a deeply profound personal experience that has inspired me throughout my 15-year spiritual journey.

It is difficult enough to convey worldly experience through words. It is infinitely more difficult, however, to put into words a spiritual experience that is not of this world. But I'll do my best to do so, trusting that there is the implicit understanding that the experience itself was far beyond anything that could ever be put into words.

When I was in my early twenties, I began meditating. The form of meditation is irrelevant, as all the true techniques have but one ultimate purpose: to lead us to connect to the truth of our being.

I understood this purpose early on. I knew that inside me existed a portal to a place of infinite love. I didn't know how I knew; I just knew. I knew that there was an infinitely loving Creator, and I wanted to connect deeply with It. I wanted this so strongly that I would often spend hours a day meditating. I would sit or even lie down in stillness and just focus within myself on a point of singularity and feel it as deeply as possible. I knew that if I was somehow able to funnel the focus of my consciousness on one point within me, then I could connect to something far beyond myself. I did this for months on end, each day with a strong desire to unite with that love that I knew existed.

Then, one day, something that is beyond the realm of explanation occurred. That day, I was meditating with the greatest focus I had ever experienced, being completely overtaken with the inner desire to "reach the Infinite." Two hours into the meditation, my body started to feel extremely light. A deeply peaceful sensation came over me, and I felt that I was floating, almost without any mass. I kept focusing on a point of singularity within myself as this was occurring, and suddenly it happened. It was as if a portal of consciousness opened up, and I "fell" through it. But it didn't feel like falling. Rather, it felt like being completely enveloped by an infinitely greater consciousness.

Suddenly, I had no sense of my physical body whatsoever. There was no sense of sound. There was nothing to see. There was nothing to touch. But it was the fullest experience one could possibly imagine. In fact, it was completely beyond imagination. What I experienced was unspeakable love and joy. A love and joy so unfathomable that nothing we ever experience as human beings even comes remotely close. And it wasn't me, Ziad, who was "feeling" this. It wasn't a mere feeling. Rather, it was a state of being in and of itself, without subject and object. Not only was I completely enveloped by this infinite ocean of limitless love and joy but also, to my utter astonishment, I *was it*. There was no me *and* it. There was no individual separate me *experiencing* it. I was it. And it was me. And it was a state of completion so full, so complete, and so utterly fulfilling that I have tears in my eyes now just writing about it.

The best analogy I can use to explain it is that of a drop of water and the ocean. Imagine yourself as a drop of water. For as long as you can remember, this drop is all that you have experienced yourself to be and all that you thought you were. And then, suddenly, someone drops you into the ocean. But instead of disappearing into the ocean, you instantaneously experience yourself as the *entire* ocean. You experience a fullness that you never knew existed. You experience a state of being so far removed from what you've known that you are in complete awe. And now imagine that this ocean is a consciousness of pure love and joy. Imagine infinite love and joy existing as an ocean that is very real, and imagine being that ocean and experiencing that joy and love as your *Self*. That is precisely what I experienced. It only lasted a few seconds because I was so amazed that thoughts quickly came in and snapped my consciousness back into this reality. But when I came back, I sprang off the couch and started literally jumping up and down with tears flowing from my eyes, saying only "thank you, thank you, thank you." All I could express was immense and profound gratitude for the experience. And that night I slept with the most incredible sense of complete peace that I have ever experienced in my life. Everything was perfect from a deep place where I knew it always would be no matter what seemed to happen in life.

As profound and mesmerizingly beautiful as that experience was, something very interesting struck me about it. Right as the portal of consciousness was opening and I was "falling" into this other realm, I had the strangest feeling. And that feeling was one of "Finally I'm back. I'm back home again." Even though I was in utter shock about how such a beatific realm could even exist, it was so incredibly familiar that it literally felt that I had been on a long journey, and I had finally returned home to a most beloved place I had all but forgotten.

Now here's where all of this starts to make wonderful sense. At the time, I didn't fully comprehend it, but now I understand it much better. You see, our true identity is completely beyond even consciousness once we get into the seventh density and above. For being conscious implies something else to be conscious *of*. But there *is* nothing else in perfect Oneness. There is only Beingness itself, self-aware. Everything we see and experience in the universe is a form of consciousness projected by this infinite Beingness so that it can experience itself in relation *to* itself and learn from the experience. We thus experience ourselves to be an individual soul that is evolving and that will reach the seventh density only in the long distant future, but because time is but an illusion, the reality is that our true Self, or what I've been calling the Spirit Self, *already* exists there.

Some of the channeled teachings tell us that we can

188

temporarily glimpse the seventh density and beyond, even while in human form. And I believe that the profound meditation experience I had was nothing more than a temporary shift in my consciousness, such that it was no longer anchored in the physical third-density body but was suddenly transported to the seventh-density reality from which it arose, thereby dissolving completely into that limitless Beingness. *That* is what I experienced as the ocean of love and joy that is so beautiful it cannot come close to being described in words. It was *myself.* My true Self, beyond the illusion of separation, in perfect Beingness with nothing else existing but pure love.

And what I'm here to remind you of, my dear brother or sister on this journey of life, is that your Self is just as beautiful. You were truly created in the image of your Creator, but that image is not this human form. The image you were created in is an image beyond all physical images. It is nothing short of infinite love and joy. And while you may also one day have the beautiful blessing of getting a temporary glimpse of it in this life, don't get hung up on that. Instead, remember your ultimate goal, which is to return home to it *permanently* and look to live your life with this overriding purpose. Live your life from a place of love toward everyone and everything, including yourself, and know that what awaits you is nothing less than infinite love and joy, forever endless.

AWAKENING PRACTICES

This simple meditation is truly profound. It's the one I was using when I had the mystical experience described in this chapter. I suggest spending more time on it than the other awakening practices; at least 20 minutes but up to an hour or more is ideal. Try not to have any expectations of what you should experience. The goal is not to duplicate my experience but to go within and connect in your own way. There are an infinite number of possibilities, so be open to anything unfolding. And even if you seem to experience nothing, just the act of focusing within in this manner awakens your consciousness and strengthens your connection to your true Self.

Before starting the meditation, silence your phone and try to make sure that you won't be disturbed. Sit or lie down in a comfortable position, close your eyes, and gently begin.

PORTAL TO THE INFINITE

Some days it's easy to focus during meditation and at other times it's difficult. Be kind to yourself and know there is value simply in the noticing of arising thoughts and responding to them with nonjudgment. Even if nothing else happens, that alone makes one hour worth a hundred years.

- Take several deep breaths, relaxing with each one, and then let your breathing return to its normal rhythm.

- Now focus all of your attention within and gently bring that attention to one spot within yourself. You can choose to focus on one small spot within your head, in your chest, or in your stomach. It doesn't matter where. The important thing is the sharp focus of attention on one place within.

- Keep your focus there as consistently as you can, trying to go deeper within yourself at that spot. You might find it helpful to think of it like finding a tunnel, and then going deeper and deeper inside. While you can visualize that if it helps, the important part is not to see anything, but to feel. Feel yourself going deeper and deeper within. If thoughts come and you find that you've strayed from your focus, simply put the focus back again on going deeper within. Don't feel bad or beat yourself up. Unless you're a monk who's been meditating for years in a cave, you will have many moments of distraction and sometimes even whole blocks of time in which you'll lose yourself in thoughts. No matter. As soon as you notice that you've lost focus, gently come back and resume your focus.

- Continue focusing on going deeper and deeper within for as long as you find it comfortable to do so, and enjoy whatever experience unfolds.

A WEEK OF AWAKENING

"Two roads diverged in a wood, and I— I
took the one less traveled by, and that
has made all the difference."

– ROBERT FROST

In this book I have endeavored to take you on a journey of awakening, removing the veil of reality and exploring the hidden structure of existence. I have also shared what I believe to be the essential practical aspect of all of this knowledge, and offered you awakening practices that I have learned and created through my own journey. It is through using these tools that this knowledge comes alive and can truly transform your life and the world you live in.

But deep transformation is not just about doing a few minutes of meditative practices and then going about your day unconsciously. The real evolution of consciousness occurs when the very lens through which you see reality changes, and your whole purpose becomes about embodying an attitude of love and kindness with yourself and others throughout the day.

Of course, Part II provided you with a lot of practical information on how to make this shift in perception into unity consciousness and live your life based on its principles. But you may have a lifetime of experience in the consciousness of the world, which is still largely based on the idea that separation is real. So to make a true and lasting shift to more of a unity consciousness and all the peace and joy that comes with it, it is very helpful to commit fully to a period of reconditioning your mind to perceive in a different way. To help you do that, I'd like to offer you the following seven-day process.

THE PROCESS

The following practices are intended to be used over a seven-day period. If you miss a day, you'll need to go back and redo the previous day you completed before continuing on to the day you missed. If you realize that you forgot to practice for most of the day, then I'd suggest redoing that day as often as you need to, and then continue with the rest.

Please note that the seven-day process is not about perfection. While we are striving to embody a consciousness of unity, we must understand that within the illusion, this human we believe ourselves to be cannot be perfect. So the goal throughout each of the days is to completely forgive yourself whenever you notice that you are not doing the process perfectly (either because you're forgetting it, ignoring it, or not being able to carry through with it). If you consistently notice these occurrences throughout the day with nonjudgmental awareness and forgive yourself, you are practicing the process, and will be ready to move on to the next day.

How to Begin Each Day

Before doing anything else, start each day with the "Embraced by the Self" (see Chapter 9 Awakening Practices) and "Embrace of Love" (see Chapter 7 Awakening Practices). Do them in that order, first connecting to your Spirit Self, and then letting that love expand outward, as specified in the practices. This gets you in the right state of mind to begin the day.

If you need to read something inspiring first to help you wake up and get into the practices, you might choose to read sections of this book (or any other book that touches your soul), or my *Sincerely, Life* blog at www.sincerelylifeblog.com, which I've written to be a guide for the journey of life. If you have the time and feel inspired to practice more, feel free to do any number of the other awakening practices from Chapters 7–10.

What to Do Throughout Each Day

In addition to doing the specific process for each day that I outline below, take one minute every waking hour to remember and reconnect with your purpose for the day, which is simply to be a vessel through which unconditional love can flow. This doesn't mean that you don't care about your work or that you neglect your responsibilities. Quite the contrary, the number one rule is to be normal and not "act spiritual," nor pretend that you don't care about the seemingly mundane things in life. Being spiritual is not about showing off our spiritual intellectualism or disdaining the physical world. Respect your work and responsibilities and do your best. Respect the illusion and act like a normal person going about his or her day. But throughout that, cultivate an inner attitude that says, "My purpose is my priority, and no matter what happens during this day, I will place my purpose first."

You may want to set an hourly alarm or reminder to take one minute per hour to reconnect with your purpose, but it is more valuable to commit to remembering it despite the busyness of the day. Having this intention allows you to be much more involved in the process and truly make it your priority. If you notice that you missed one or more hourly reconnection intervals, don't beat yourself up or toss the rest of the day aside because you feel you failed. To the contrary, forgive yourself with gentle kindness and carry on. At the end of the day you can decide whether to move on or redo the day. Also, if you have the time and privacy and feel so inclined, you can go beyond the minute and do one or more of the awakening practices from Chapters 7–10.

How to End Each Day

Whatever happened during the day, and no matter how well or poorly you think you performed in upholding your deeper purpose, close the day by treating yourself with utmost compassion, remembering that you are in a classroom and that learning naturally entails mistakes. Recommit to living your purpose the next day, and use one or more of the awakening practices from Chapters 7–10 before going to bed, so that you fall sleep from a place of strength and peace, and rise the next day with a renewed sense of purpose.

Day 1

Today is about being in appreciation for everything in your life. Go through the entire day in a state of gratitude, seeking the good in everyone and everything that happens, and internally expressing appreciation for it. Try to feel the most gratitude for the seemingly negative things that happen, no matter how small or big, for they are your greatest catalysts for transformation. It's easy to be thankful and appreciate the good. It's a whole other thing to do that with the seemingly bad—which is precisely why it's such an incredible catalyst of true growth.

DAY 2

Today is about unconditional acceptance and nonresistance to what is, including resistance itself. Go through the entire day in a state of mindfulness and acceptance, welcoming what is. Welcome all the events that occur (whether they are seemingly good or bad), any physical discomfort or pain, as well as all thoughts and emotions. Notice how you want to instinctively resist anything that you perceive as negative (whether it's external, physical, mental, or emotional), and welcome and accept even that resistance. This means that if you find that you are resisting something, don't fight it (which is merely more resistance), but welcome it too.

DAY 3

Today is about keeping the perspective that everything that occurs is for your ultimate good, chosen wisely by your Spirit Self to offer yourself the greatest catalysts for soul evolution. Go through the entire day seeing everyone and everything as your teacher. Keep the perspective that you chose all your learning catalysts before you took physical incarnation in this lifetime. This means that you are never a victim. No matter what is happening, good or bad, big or small, your Spirit Self chose it from a higher level, knowing that it is for your ultimate good. Remember that with every interaction and event that happens today.

Day 4

Today is about looking beyond appearances to see and have compassion for the fearful and hurting child within yourself and everyone. Go through the day seeing your own and everyone else's inner child. In every interaction you have today, especially any upsetting ones (whether with someone you know or with other drivers in traffic, for example), choose to see beyond appearances to the hurt child within. Literally visualize each person as a small child who is in fear and pain, and mentally offer them your compassion.

Do this with yourself too. Anytime someone does something that brings up a negative emotion (or a circumstance that triggers it, even without an interaction with another person), see the hurt child within yourself whose old pain is being triggered by the present event, and offer that child love and compassion. This means that if you happen to react unconsciously and end up hurting someone with your words or actions, instead of judging yourself see your hurt inner child lashing out and offer it the love it needs.

Day 5

Today is a day to see the truth of everyone's being behind the veil. Go through the day seeing everyone as their Spirit Self. While their physical self may say or do something that hurts you, remember that this isn't who they truly are. They are radiant nonphysical beings made of pure love, and their physical self is one of the catalysts through which they chose to learn—and offer to others to learn from as well. Be thankful for the lessons that they offer you, while seeing the truth of their being behind the physical form.

DAY 6

Today is a day to remember that you are the universe experiencing itself from infinite perspectives, and everyone you come across is actually you in a different temporary form. Go through the day seeing everyone as you. Keep reminding yourself of the true physics of reality that you learned in this book, and see everyone not as limited by their physical body, but as energy that has chosen to become seemingly solidified, but which still extends beyond the physical body at one with everything, including you. In fact it's not just at one with you, but from the higher level of ultimate reality, it *is* you. On this day, love each of those aspects of you, no matter how they seem to be acting within the illusion.

DAY 7

Today is a day of embodying unconditional love itself. Go through the day as love itself embracing everyone and everything. Remember that beyond all illusions, the only thing that exists is infinite love. Channel that love today. Be an instrument for it to envelop and flow through, and perceive yourself not as the body and personality you think yourself to be, but as love itself, wanting nothing but to give of itself. Each time you notice that you have shifted back to the perspective of the physical personality, gently embody the love and see through its eyes. How would love think? How would it speak? How would it treat others, including the physical you? Today, you find out.

A LIFE OF AWAKENING

If you've gone through the weeklong awakening process, you've surely had a transformative experience filled with many moments of love, joy, peace, and awe. If you'd like life to be like this from now on, the key is not to use this weeklong practice as a one-off and then return to the previous way of living. Rather, realize that this can be every week. Indeed, awakening is not a destination. It is a beautiful unending process that takes you deeper and deeper into the heart of eternity, which is your true Self.

So if your heart has resonated with this process, listen to its call and commit to making it a way of life. Make this week, every week. Look at it as a cycle to continue, with each new turn bringing greater and greater awakening of consciousness. Seen in this way, you don't have to take a pilgrimage or sit in a cave for years to attain spiritual enlightenment. Rather, your very life becomes the curriculum of your higher learning. You live a normal life in the world, but you live it from beyond the veil.

You don't have to follow the exact weekly process I've presented here. You can choose to do it in whatever way feels right to your soul. If you resonated with one or more of the daily processes more than the others, focus on those. If one in particular was very powerful and worked quite effectively for you, feel free to make that your daily practice and the lens through which you view the world. The specific content doesn't matter, as it all leads to living the awakened life. And that life becomes the masterpiece that you offer all beings, in service to the One Infinite Loving Creator. And what life could be better lived than that?

All my love to you on this beautiful journey.

REFERENCES

1. Panek, Richard. 2011. *The 4 Percent Universe: Dark Matter, Dark Energy, and the Race to Discover the Rest of Reality.* Mariner Books

2. https://en.wikipedia.org/wiki/Double-slit_experiment

3. http://education.jlab.org/qa/how-much-of-an-atom-is-empty-space.html

4. http://www.symmetrymagazine.org/article/the-particle-physics-of-you

5. Kuhn, Greg. 2013. *Why Quantum Physicists Create More Abundance.* Greg Kuhn

6. Swan, Teal. 2015. *Shadows Before Dawn: Finding the Light of Self-Love Through Your Darkest Times.* Hay House

7. Wilcock, David. 2011. *The Source Field Investigations: The Hidden Sciences and Lost Civilizations Behind the 2012 Prophecies.* New York: Dutton

8. Folger, Tim. *Discover Magazine*, December 2001: 22 (9)

9. Planck, Max. 1944. "Das Wesen der Materie" ("The Nature of Matter"), speech delivered in Florence, Italy: Archiv zur Geschichte der Max-Planck-Gesellschaft, Abt. Va, Rep. 11 Planck, Nr. 1797

10. Conn Henry, Richard. 2005. "The Mental Universe." *Nature*: 436(29)

11. Backster, Cleve. 2003. *Primary Perception: Biocommunication with Plants, Living Foods, and Human Cells.* Anza, CA: White Rose Millennium Press.

12. Tompkins, Peter; Bird, Christopher. 1989. *The Secret Life of Plants: A Fascinating Account of the Physical, Emotional, and*

Spiritual Relations between Plants and Man. New York: Perennial.

13. Stevenson, Ian. 2001. *Children Who Remember Previous Lives: A Question of Reincarnation*. Jefferson, NC: McFarland.

14. Tucker, Jim. B. 2005. *Life Before Life: Children's Memories of Previous Lives*. New York: St. Martin's Press.

15. _____. 2013. *Return to Life: Extraordinary Cases of Children Who Remember Past Lives*. New York: St. Martin's Press.

16. Stevenson, Ian. 1992. "Birthmarks and Birth Defects Corresponding to Wounds on Deceased Persons," paper presented at the Eleventh Annual Meeting of the Society for Scientific Exploration, Princeton University, June 11–13

17. Newton, Michael. 1994. *Journey of Souls: Case Studies of Life between Lives*. St. Paul, MN: Llewellyn

18. _____. 2000. *Destiny of Souls: New Case Studies of Life between Lives*. St. Paul, MN: Llewellyn.

19. Weiss, Brian. 1988. *Many Lives, Many Masters*. New York: Simon & Schuster

20. Cannon, Delores. 2013. *Between Death and Life: Conversations with a Spirit*. Ozark Mountain Publishing.

21. http://www.huffingtonpost.com/george-musser/space-time-illusion_b_9703656.html

22. Moody, Raymond A. 2001. *Life After Life*. New York: HarperCollins

23. International Association for Near Death Studies. 2015. "What Is a Near-Death Experience?" Last updated: July 8 2015. http://iands.org/ndes/about-ndes/what-is-an-nde.html

24. Alexander, Eben. 2012. *Proof of Heaven: A Neurosurgeon's Journey into the Afterlife*. New York: Simon & Schuster

25. http://science.time.com/2013/11/04/so-much-for-earth-being-special-there-could-be-20-billion-just-like-it/

26. Pratt, David. 1997. "The Last Pyramid." Last updated: August 2010. http://www.davidpratt.info/pyramid.htm

27. Browne, Sylvia. 2006. *Secrets and Mysteries of the World*. Hay House

28. http://www.ancient-code.com/25-facts-about-the-great-pyramid-of-giza/

29. http://science.nationalgeographic.com/science/archaeology/nasca-lines/

30. http://www.ibtimes.co.uk/worlds-biggest-monolithic-stone-block-discovered-baalbek-roman-sanctuary-lebanon-1478792

31. https://www.theguardian.com/film/2011/sep/29/mayan-documentary-alien-mexico

32. http://www.ancient-code.com/the-dogon-tribe-connection-sirius/

33. Umana, John. 2005. *Creation: Towards a Theory of All Things*. Booksurge Publishing

34. http://www.cropcirclesecrets.org/radioactive.html

35. Interview with Yolanda Gaskins for the television show *Paranormal Borderline*, aired May 9, 1996

36. https://www.youtube.com/watch?v=BF8eztsVr40

37. https://www.youtube.com/watch?v=nWTldrEYsoE

38. https://www.youtube.com/watch?v=TqahF0nb7rM

39. Oberth, Hermann. 1954. "Flying Saucers Come from a Distant World" published in the Sunday newspaper supplement "The American Weekly".

40. Thrive documentary. 2011. Clear Compass Media

41. First Contact documentary. 2016. Zia Films

42. Elkins, Don; McCarty, James Allen; Rueckert, Carla. 1984. *The Ra Material: An Ancient Astronaut Speaks*. Whitford Press

43. Bush, Nancy Evans. 2012. *Dancing Past the Dark: Distressing Near-Death Experiences*. Seattle: Amazon Digital Services

44. Wilcock, David. 2016. *The Ascension Mysteries: Revealing the Cosmic Battle between Good and Evil*. New York: Dutton

45. _____. 2013. *The Synchronicity Key*: The Hidden Intelligence Guiding the Universe and You. New York: Dutton

46. Rieske, Kent. R. 2016. "Top Ten Scientific Facts Proving Charles Darwin's Theory of Evolution Is Wrong, False, and Impossible." Accessed October 20, 2016. http://www.biblelife.org/evolution.htm

47. Solar Revolution. 2012. Screen Addiction

48. http://www.bbc.com/earth/story/20160318-why-there-might-be-many-more-universes-besides-our-own

49. https://en.wikipedia.org/wiki/Repetition_compulsion